DIG IN

THE DEVOTED WARRIOR

RON LUCE

Author of *Battle Cry for a Generation*

NE✝GEN®

Building the New Generation of Believers

COOK COMMUNICATIONS MINISTRIES
Colorado Springs, Colorado • Paris, Ontario
KINGSWAY COMMUNICATIONS LTD
Eastbourne, England

NexGen® is an imprint of
Cook Communications Ministries
Colorado Springs, CO 80918
Cook Communications, Paris, Ontario
Kingsway Communications, Eastbourne, England

DIG IN: THE DEVOTED WARRIOR LEADER'S GUIDE
© 2006 by Ron Luce

The Word at Work Around the World

A vital part of Cook Communications Ministries is our international outreach, Cook Communications International (CCMI). Your purchase of this book, and of other books and Christian-growth products from Cook, enables CCMI to provide Bibles and Christian literature to people in more than 150 languages in 65 countries.

First Printing, 2006
Printed in Canada
                  1 2 3 4 5 6 7 8 9 10 Printing/Year 10 09 08 07 06

Written by David and Kelli Trujillo
Cover Design: Marks & Whetstone
Interior Design: Helen Harrison

ISBN 0-78144-436-5

TABLE OF CONTENTS

Acknowledgments 4

Letter from Ron Luce 5

Minute-by-Minute Weekend Schedule 6

Minute-by-Minute Weekly Schedule 7

Scheduling Options...8

Getting Prepped for *Dig In* 10

It's *Go* Time: How to Navigate the Experience 13

Master Supply List 16

Session 1: Devoted to the King 17

Session 2: True Power, Total Authority 31

Session 3: I'm Yours Forever! 45

Session 4: Defying the Enemy 61

Session 5: His Agents 75

Session 6: Courage Under Fire 91

Session 7: Retreat Is Not an Option 107

Leader's Guide Endnotes...124

The Next Step: Youth Leader Follow-Up...........................125

ACKNOWLEDGMENTS

I would like to thank David and Kelli Trujillo, Missy Wetzel, Sharron Jackson, and the many others with Cook Communications who helped pull everything together.

A special thanks to the Center for Creative Media Team including Doug Rittenhouse, Greg Williams, and Heath Hicks for putting together the media tools and to Steelehouse for their creativity with the video content.

DIG IN LEADER'S GUIDE

> THE MEN who followed Him were unique in their generation. They turned the world upside-down because their hearts had been turned right side up. The world has never been the same.
>
> —Billy Graham

Dear Youth Specialist,

The battle cry has sounded. This generation is under attack, and a half-hearted skirmish will not cut it! It's not enough for teens to go to church on Sundays, stop by youth group on Wednesdays, and buy into the enemy's lies every other day of the week.

It's time to equip young people for battle, and it's time to send our youth to the front lines in the fight against lies and darkness. It's time for this generation to take a stand for Jesus Christ!

What you have in your hands is part of a national movement among Christian youth toward the things of God. This is a unique moment for each person in your youth group to get serious about impacting his generation. It's time for your teens to *Dig In* . . . to the Word, to the character of God, and to the lifestyle of a warrior.

Dig In: The Devoted Warrior will be a life-transforming experience for every person in your youth group. Teens will discover the true, divine nature of God. They will understand, perhaps for the first time, the magnitude of Christ's sacrifice. And they will be challenged to live a life of devotion, defiance, and courage!

You have everything you will need to use *Dig In: The Devoted Warrior* as a powerful weekend experience or a seven-week series. The kit includes 10 Training Manuals for teens, a detailed Leader's Guide, a sample of the follow-up self-discipleship resource *Over the Edge: Ultimate Submission,* and a contemporary, relevant DVD packed full of videos illustrating each lesson. Other helpful resources and promotional materials can be accessed online at http://downloads.battlecry.com.

Even with all that is provided, *Dig In's* impact on your teens cannot be scripted. There is no telling what the Lord will do with open hearts. This is a time to let Him move. He wants to work powerfully in and through your youth group. He wants your teens to turn this world upside-down!

Thank you for all the sacrifices you make for your youth and for the Kingdom.
God bless you!

Consumed by the Call,
Ron Luce
President and Founder
Battle Cry Movement/Acquire the Fire youth conventions

MINUTE-BY-MINUTE WEEKEND SCHEDULE

FRIDAY NIGHT

5:00 p.m.	Dinner (optional)
6:00 p.m.	Begin Session 1: "Devoted to the King" (including Optional Warm-Up Activity)
8:00 p.m.	End Session 1 15-minute break/optional snack (let your group know to be back at 8:15)
8:15 p.m.	Begin Session 2: "True Power, Total Authority"
9:45 p.m.	End Session 2 End of the night

SATURDAY MORNING

7:30 a.m.	Breakfast
8:15 a.m.	Worship (optional)
8:30 a.m.	Begin Session 3: "I'm Yours Forever!" (including Optional Warm-Up Activity)
10:30 a.m.	End Session 3 15-minute break/optional snack (let your group know to be back at 10:45)
10:45 a.m.	Begin Session 4: "Defying the Enemy"
12:15 p.m.	End Session 4
12:30 p.m.	Lunch

SATURDAY AFTERNOON

1:15 p.m.	Begin Session 5: "His Agents" (including Optional Warm-Up Activity)
3:15 p.m.	End Session 5 15-minute break/optional snack (let your group know to be back at 3:30)
3:30 p.m.	Begin Session 6: "Courage under Fire"
5:00 p.m.	End Session 6, Dinner (optional)
6:00 p.m.	Begin Session 7: "Retreat is Not an Option" (including Optional Warm-Up Activity)
8:00 p.m.	End Session 7

MINUTE-BY-MINUTE WEEKLY SCHEDULE

WEEK 1

30 min.	Session 1's Optional Warm-Up Activity
90 min.	Session 1: "Devoted to the King"
15 min.	Snack (optional)

WEEK 2

30 min.	Session 2's Optional Warm-Up Activity
90 min.	Session 2: "True Power, Total Authority"
15 min.	Snack (optional)

WEEK 3

30 min.	Session 3's Optional Warm-Up Activity
90 min.	Session 3: "I'm Yours Forever!"
15 min.	Snack (optional)

WEEK 4

30 min.	Session 4's Optional Warm-Up Activity
90 min.	Session 4: "Defying the Enemy"
15 min.	Snack (optional)

WEEK 5

30 min.	Session 5's Optional Warm-Up Activity
90 min.	Session 5: "His Agents"
15 min.	Snack (optional)

WEEK 6

30 min.	Session 6's Optional Warm-Up Activity
90 min.	Session 6: "Courage under Fire"
15 min.	Snack (optional)

WEEK 7

30 min.	Session 7's Optional Warm-Up Activity
90 min.	Session 7: "Retreat is Not an Option"
15 min.	Snack (optional)

WEEKEND OPTIONS:
LODGING ARRANGEMENTS

We encourage you to structure this intense weekend experience as a retreat or lock-in at your church facility or off-campus at a camp or retreat center. You also have the option to send students home after the first two sessions on Friday night and then reconvene on Saturday morning. If your group spends the night on location, you may choose to lead structured activities at 10 p.m. or give teens low-key free time until bed. "Lights-out" time is up to you.

FOOD

Meals: Saturday's breakfast and lunch are the only required meals. You may choose to have students arrive early on Friday evening and/or stay late on Saturday for dinner. Gathering for meals is an excellent opportunity for teens and leaders to experience authentic relationship. We suggest that you plan something that is easy but also shows you have put thought into it. Your budget, group size, and volunteer base will all determine what meals work best for you.

Dinner and lunch ideas: lasagna (the pre-made frozen pans work great!), pizza, sub sandwich bar, burgers and/or hot dogs on the grill, or taco bar.

Breakfast ideas: pancakes, eggs, and bacon; bagels and cream cheese; or donuts and juice.

Snacks: During each of the four short breaks, have snacks and drinks available. We suggest quick, easy options such as bottled water and juices, candy bars, fruit snacks, veggies and dip, or cookies. Keep in mind that these breaks are only 15 minutes long.

WORSHIP

In addition to worship within the sessions themselves, you'll find an optional worship time in Saturday's schedule. Don't feel limited, however, to this slot. If you feel the Spirit prompting a time of song and prayer, go for it! Choose songs that most of your group is familiar with. If you have worship musicians available, make arrangements with them ahead of time. Worship CDs will also work.

WEEKLY OPTIONS:
GROUP SIZE
Dig In:The Devoted Warrior works for large and small groups alike. From a small group of 3-12 meeting at their leader's home to a group of hundreds meeting in their church's worship center, weekly *Dig In* sessions can be life altering for everyone involved!

SNACKS
Each session ends with an optional snack time. This snack time gives leaders and students an informal opportunity to discuss and process the evening's lesson. We suggest quick, easy snack options such as bottled water and juices, candy bars, fruit snacks, veggies and dip, or cookies.

WORSHIP
In addition to worship within the sessions themselves, you can also feel free to add more worship time to the event's schedule. If you feel the Spirit prompting a time of song and prayer, go for it! Choose songs that most of your group is familiar with. If you have worship musicians available, make arrangements with them ahead of time. Worship CDs will also work.

GETTING PREPPED FOR DIG IN

PUBLICITY

Dig In: The Devoted Warrior is a one-of-a-kind discipleship experience. You want as many teens to know about it as possible! So take advantage of some of these publicity ideas.

Log on to http://downloads.battlecry.com and download the following for free:

POSTERS. Display these in your youth room, around your church, and in your community. Be sure to fill in the specifics regarding your event.

BULLETIN INSERTS. Hand these out at your church services, Sunday school classes, and youth group events. Fill in the specific details for your event.

POSTCARDS. Fill in the specifics and send them out to each teen on your mailing list.

CLIP-ART GRAPHICS. Use these images to create your own fliers, bulletin inserts, web page ad, newsletter announcement, and e-mail blasts.

Encourage your students to invite their Christian friends from school and work.

Check your records for the names of every teen who has been a part of your group, whether presently or in the past. Make it a point to personally invite each one. You can use the postcards at http://downloads.battlecry.com or make phone calls. This is a great opportunity to involve other adult leaders and volunteers.

LEADER'S LOW-DOWN:

It's best if students bring their own Bibles to *Dig In: The Devoted Warrior*. Be sure to mention this in your publicity. You also will want to have extra Bibles on hand for students who either don't have their own or simply forgot to bring them.

ADULT LEADERS

You will want to recruit and include other adult leaders in this experience. If you already have a team of leaders (adult volunteers, college students, parents, etc.), it's important to get them involved through prayer and participation in the lessons. Invite them to attend the sessions and ask them to be available for individual prayer and ministry. You may even choose to have other adults participate in facilitating some of the sessions through reading Scripture or leading discussions. Adult leaders can also help with publicity, décor, and food preparation prior to the event. During basic training, volunteers can welcome students, facilitate small groups, help with set-up and clean-up between activities, and lead games. At all stages of this experience, prayer is key. Ask a group of adults to provide a prayer covering over your group and facility before, during, and after *Dig In* (see description below).

Invite your ministry team to a training meeting a week or two prior to the start of *Dig In*. Help them understand the purpose of this discipleship experience and walk them through the schedule. Provide any additional training that you feel is needed. For example, adult volunteers may need help knowing how to lead students into a relationship with Christ or how to facilitate discussions and ask open-ended questions. Encourage your leaders to prepare their own hearts before the event by setting personal time aside for prayer and Scripture reading.

PRAYER

Gather a group of willing adults from your church to pray for the entire *Dig In* experience. This prayer group can help in a number of powerful ways:

• They can meet regularly (once a week or every day) during the weeks before the event. They can pray for each student attending (provide them with an updated list of names each time), the facility, and the leaders.
• They can meet while the event is taking place.
• Adults can sign up for an hour of prayer on their own. A group prayer schedule can cover the days before, during, and after the event.
• Use the clip-art graphics at http://downloads.battlecry.com to create prayer bookmarks. Each student can write his name on a bookmark and give it to an adult in the church during a Sunday service prior to the event. Adults will then commit to pray for the students on their bookmarks.
• Involve your senior pastor. Ask him to announce the *Dig In* event during the church service and encourage the congregation to pray.
• Follow up after *Dig In* with your prayer team and congregation, letting them know all the exciting things God did during *Dig In*.

FACILITY

The size of your group will determine how large of a room you need. You may use your youth room, sanctuary, or an off-site facility such as a camp or conference center. A large free-standing wooden cross should be the focal point of your meeting room. Students will utilize this cross in worship at the conclusion of most of the sessions. Make sure there is room around the cross to allow space for teenagers to gather around it. As you read through the sessions ahead of time, take note of any needed room adjustments.

While most of *Dig In* is designed for an indoor setting, many of the games and activities will also work well outdoors.

Here are some ideas for making your facility inviting:

DRAW FOOTPRINTS (perhaps in the shape of a boot bottom) leading to your room. You can use sidewalk chalk outside and tape or large paper inside.

PROJECT CLIP-ART IMAGES (from http://downloads.battlecry.com) onto the walls to create large posters to hang around the meeting room.

USE MILITARY PARAPHERNALIA to decorate the room. From uniforms to posters to rucksacks and combat boots. (Check out your local military surplus store or ask members of your church who serve in the military.) Make the room look like a real boot camp.

FORMS

Students may bring friends who have never before been to your youth group, so make sure you have information cards available. If you do not already have standard cards that you use, you may want to create a small form the size of an index card that students fill out. Make sure to include space for their name, address, phone number, parents' names, e-mail, school, and name of the friend who invited them. You may also want a medical release and permission form especially if you plan on transporting teens during *Dig In*.

THE NEXT STEP

A key to the continued effect of *Dig In: The Devoted Warrior* is ongoing discipleship. Included in the kit is a preview copy of *Over the Edge: Ultimate Submission,* a seven-week daily study designed to guide students in taking what they learned and experienced during *Dig In* and applying it day in and day out. *Ultimate Submission* bridges youth from the training stage to the frontline battle. Become familiar with it; you will have a chance in the last session to introduce this next step. *Ultimate Submission* equips each student to have a unique, individual experience, so you may choose to order a copy for each member of your youth group at Battlecry.com. If resources are limited, you may instead choose to invite teens or their parents to each order a copy. You can download a parent letter at http://downloads.battlecry.com. Be sure to fill in your specific information.

Over the Edge: Ultimate Submission is primarily an independent self-discipleship experience for each of your teens. However, they will gain maximum benefit only if you and other leaders provide accountability. You will find specific follow-up suggestions on pages 125-128. The more practical reinforcement of *Dig In*'s lessons that your youth receive, the more they will be equipped to be change-agents for Christ in their schools, homes, and community!

IT'S GO TIME: HOW TO NAVIGATE THE EXPERIENCE

Dig In: The Devoted Warrior is a youth group experience written specifically with Christian teens in mind. As a discipleship tool, it will challenge your teens to a radical, Christian lifestyle. It has been written with the assumption that the teens going through this experience have already committed their lives to the Lord and have at least a basic understanding of the Bible. It is likely, however, that there will be teens present who have not yet made personal decisions for Jesus Christ. This is a discipleship experience, so you don't want to dilute the message for the sake of nonbelievers. Yet, be sensitive to those who do not yet know Jesus personally. Encourage nonbelievers to stay and learn what it looks like to follow Christ.

STRUCTURING BASIC TRAINING

Dig In: The Devoted Warrior has been written in a unique format that you can use either as an intense weekend youth group event (Friday night through Saturday evening) or as a seven-week small- or large-group experience. You'll find schedules and scheduling options shown in detail on pages 6-9.

UNDERSTANDING THIS LEADER'S GUIDE

THE SCRIPT

Within each session, all text in bold is for you to say to your group. Look for the **SAY:** and **ASK:** symbols; they indicate that the following words are to be read out loud. All non-bolded text gives you specific instructions that are not to be read out loud to your group.

Though scripted words have been provided, always remember that you know your group best! You have the freedom to follow the text verbatim or to use the script as a springboard for expressing your own thoughts and examples.

THE ICONS

 You will find two major icons throughout each session.

Indicates that students will be looking at or working in their Training Manuals.

 Points out when a DVD clip is used.

"A QUICK GLANCE"

You will find "A Quick Glance" box at the start of each session. This feature gives you a brief rundown of the session's contents. You will see the titles, supply lists, and approximate time frames for each section.

Remember that time frames given for each section are approximate. Feel free to lengthen, shorten, or even eliminate activities based on the flow and dynamics of your specific group.

"LEADER'S LOW-DOWN"

These boxes are filled with helpful tips and suggestions.

"SHORT SYNOPSIS"

This feature gives you a brief summary of each DVD clip.

Short Synopsis:
"Spiritopia #1"
This clip shows teens
that committing every
part of their lives to
Christ is only the begin-
ning of a difficult, exhila-
rating journey.

PLANNING AHEAD...

Whether you decide to use *Dig In:The Devoted Warrior* as a weekend event or series of seven meetings, you will want to review every session along with the teen Training Manual (it is also a good idea to keep a copy for yourself to use during your teaching time) and the DVD clips several times before you teach them. When teaching you may not want to read all of the text verbatim, but study it well and customize it for your group. Make notes in the margin and highlight words and sentences that will help cue you along the way.

You will want to prepare for activities and get supplies beforehand. Use the Master Supply List on page 16 as a guide. (Some supplies may need to be purchased.) The material list is extensive, and it will require a good amount of preparatory work to flow smoothly. Be aware that the session lengths can vary, so try to let parents and teens know what to expect ahead of time.

Each session begins with an Optional Warm-Up activity; here you'll find either a fun get-to-know-you icebreaker, an upbeat game, or an interactive affirmation activity. Though these activities are optional, they are designed to relate directly to the teaching theme of each session, so if you have time be sure to include them.

USING THE TRAINING MANUALS . . .

Included with *Dig In: The Devoted Warrior* are 10 copies of the Training Manuals for teens. Each member of your group needs an individual copy. You are invited to order additional copies from Battlecry.com. Please note that every page in the Training Manual is used at some point during the program, and every session contains corresponding journaling activities in the manual. Please remind your students that they will need their manuals for each session. Journaling is a very important part of their *Dig In* experience.

WORSHIPING DURING RISE UP . . .

Worship is a key ingredient to this impactful experience. There are worship experiences within each of the sessions that go outside the box, using prayer and symbolic activities to help students cement their commitments. During these times, you can play a worship music CD, or you may want to ask musicians to play worship music quietly in the background. If you have a youth worship leader or band, be aware that their involvement may keep them from participating in the ministry times. If this is the case, you may want to play a worship CD so that every teen can worship God and get their hearts ready to receive from Him. Make plans ahead of time in order to make these times of worship a natural extension of the lessons your teens will be learning. Don't feel limited to the scheduled worship times. Follow the Spirit's leading to sing and pray, even if it isn't part of your well-laid-out plans.

FACILITATING MINISTRY TIME . . .

Times of ministry have been strategically placed at the end of each session. These are intended to give your teens a real experience with God and allow Him to speak directly to their hearts. Be ready to lead your group where God wants to take them during these ministry opportunities.

PLAYING DVD CLIPS . . .

You will need a TV (or projector) and DVD player for all seven sessions. Turn off the TV (or projector) between videos but keep the DVD player on. Most of the clips used in *Dig In: The Devoted Warrior* are included in the DVD (with the exception of one clip used in Session One and one used in Session Three.) You will want to have the specific lesson sub-menu playing so that you can quickly access all clips for that lesson.

GIVING TEENS INDIVIDUAL ATTENTION . . .

It is important that you keep an eye on the individual needs of the students in your group. Some of your teens may require extra attention and ministry as you address various topics, which will require that you and other leaders are available after the sessions.

DOWNLOADING NAME TAGS . . .

You can download dog-tag styled name tags for free at http://downloads.battlecry.com. Name tags help develop a sense of community for the students and leaders. And if everyone is wearing one, it becomes a pretty cool thing to do!

MASTER SUPPLY LIST

FOR ALL SEVEN SESSIONS, YOU WILL NEED:

- The Leader's Guide (you will need to make a copy of Session Five for another leader during the gender-specific time)
- *Dig In* DVD, a DVD player, and a TV or projector
- A Training Manual for each member of your group
- Pencils or pens
- Lots of blank white paper
- Markers
- Extra Bibles (for those who didn't bring their own)
- A free-standing wooden cross in the front and center of your meeting room
- A worship CD and CD player. (You may instead choose to have a worship leader or band lead your group in song.)

Additional supplies are needed for specific sessions:

SESSION ONE:

- (Optional Warm-Up Activity: slips of paper)
- *The Lord of the Rings—The Return of the King* Extended Version DVD

SESSION TWO:

- (Optional Warm-Up Activity: several rolls of masking tape; blue, white, and pink index cards. Every teen gets one of each color.)
- Paper
- Several video game controllers
- Several dog leashes and collars
- A quantity of clay or play-dough

SESSION THREE:

- (Optional Warm-Up Activity: large paper bags, Symbol Scavenger Hunt sheets,

additional objects—see Leader's Low-Down box on p. 47)
- *The Count of Monte Cristo* DVD
- Images of corporate logos
- (Optional: computer with PowerPoint, projector)
- Nails (one for each teen)
- Hammers

SESSION FOUR:

- Black and red paper hearts (Every teen gets one of each.)
- 2 large newsprint banners
- (Optional: pop culture and sports magazines)
- Masking tape

SESSION FIVE:

- (Optional Warm-Up Activity: toothpicks, gumdrops, paper cups, masking tape, aluminum foil, mini-marshmallows, cloth sheet, paper bags)
- Slips of paper, prepared in advance (see directions on p. 76)
- "The World's Values/God's Values" newsprint sheet from Session Four
- Photocopies of maps (one per student)

SESSION SIX:

- Several large newsprint banners
- Candles with drip guards
- Basket
- Matches
- (Optional: Darrell Evan's CD *Trading My Sorrows: The Best of Darrell Evans*)

SESSION SEVEN:

- (Optional Warm-Up Activity: yarn, pieces of cardstock, prepared in advance (see p. 108), upbeat CD)
- Plastic bins or shoeboxes
- Potting soil
- Seeds
- Third Day's *Offerings II* CD and CD player
- (Optional: Copies of *Over the Edge: Ultimate Submission*—one for each teen)

SESSION ONE: DEVOTED TO THE KING

WHAT'S THE POINT?

God wants complete devotion from us, naming Him as Lord and King of our lives.

A QUICK GLANCE...

MINUTES	SECTION	SUPPLIES
up to 30	Optional Warm-Up Activity	Slips of paper, pens
20 to 25	Democracy or Monarchy?	Training Manuals, paper, pens, tape
20 to 25	"Lord" Isn't Just a Nickname...	Training Manuals, Bibles, Dig In DVD, TV, DVD player
15 to 20	Swearing the Oath	Training Manuals, Bibles, TV, DVD player, Lord of the Rings—The Return of the King Extended Version DVD
20 to 25	Modern Warriors	Training Manuals, Bibles, Dig In DVD, TV, DVD player
up to 10	Ministry Time	A cross up front, worship CD and CD player or an instrumentalist
up to 5	Make It Real	Training Manuals

Before the event begins, make sure you've got a Training Manual for every student. Set up a large, free-standing wooden cross near the front of your meeting area and ready a CD player with worshipful, instrumental music. Set up a TV and DVD player and be ready to play the *Dig In* DVD.

During this session, you will also play *The Lord of the Rings—The Return of the King* Extended Version DVD cued to approximately 01:19:55 when the scene opens with Peregrin sitting on a bench. He says to himself, "What were you thinking, Peregrin Took..."

OPTIONAL WARM-UP ACTIVITY

LEADER'S LOW-DOWN:

We want *Dig In: The Devoted Warrior* to be the most impactful experience possible for your group, so remember that you have the freedom to direct your youth in whatever way is best. The time frames given for each activity, for example, are approximate. Feel free to lengthen, shorten, or even eliminate activities based on the flow and dynamics of your specific group. You may choose to follow the scripted words verbatim, or you may decide to use the script as a springboard for incorporating your own thoughts and examples. You may also need to make specific arrangements based on your facility. Perhaps some activities will take place outdoors or in a larger room. Keep this in mind as you are planning.

Welcome teenagers as they arrive and have them break into teams of six to ten students for this fun get-to-know-you game. Give each student a slip of paper and a pen and have teams find their own spot in the room and sit in a circle on the floor. Explain that you are going to ask a question and that all of the students should privately write answers on their slips of paper. Let them know that they do *not* have to answer honestly—they can make up any silly answer they choose! Also, clarify that they should *not* write their names on their slips of paper.

Once everyone in a group has written an answer, a volunteer in the group should collect all the slips. He or she should read all the answers aloud while everyone else in the group listens. Then, one by one, students should go around the circle and each make one guess about who said what. (For example, "Tom, did you say peanut butter and pickles?" Tom must honestly answer "yes" or "no.") Each time a student makes a correct guess, he or she gets one point. Students in a group should keep guessing until everyone's answer has been correctly identified. Whoever has the most points is the winner.

When everyone understands, ask this first question:
- **If you could create a pizza that represented your personality, what toppings would it have on it?**

Encourage students to play several rounds of the game as time allows, each time coming up with one of their own questions. If students need ideas, have them ask a question like…
- **If you could have one super power, what would it be?**
- **If a novel was written about your life, what would its title be?**
- **Which animal best represents your personality?**

When about 10 minutes are left, direct all groups to use this question for their final round:
- **If you were a king or queen of a country, what would you name it?**

After the game, have everyone grab a Training Manual and a chair and take a seat. (Have students create rows with their chairs, facing the front of the room.)

DEMOCRACY OR MONARCHY?

Divide the group into teams of three to five and give each group paper and pens. Have everyone turn to page three in their Training Manuals and read along as you give these instructions.

SAY: You've just been put in charge of a land with one million inhabitants and have been given the job of immediately drawing up a plan for how this nation will be run. What kind of government will you put in place? What will be the laws of the land? Your job is to work together in your team to quickly write a short "constitution" that covers these four issues:

1) What type of government will you have: a monarchy, a democracy, a communist republic, or some other type of government?

2) What is the most important law of the land?

3) What will be the most important rights of citizens in your country?

4) What will be your policy toward war? Will you have a draft or a volunteer army?

You've got just 10 minutes to decide on these questions and write impromptu constitutions. Ready? Go!

LEADER'S LOW-DOWN:

If your group is made up mostly of younger teenagers, they might need some help thinking through the issues for their made-up constitution. Enlist adult volunteers to wander from group to group and help them think through the various directions they could go with each question. And if kids take their constitution in a silly direction, that's fine! Let them have fun and make it their own.

Give students 10 minutes, then have them hang up their constitutions on a wall in your meeting area. Read aloud excerpts of what some of the groups wrote.

Then **SAY: History has taught us many things. Among its lessons lies an important question concerning national authority: Who should have the final say? Is the king the seat of ultimate authority, like in a monarchy? Does the authority lie with a select privileged few, like in an oligarchy? Or, does authority lie in the people of the nation, like in a democracy?**

Write these questions on the board or have the teens jot them down. Then have students turn to a partner to discuss them.

ASK: What are the responsibilities of a citizen in a monarchy? What are the responsibilities of a citizen in a democracy? In your opinion, which type of government is best? Why?

When pairs are done, invite volunteers to share their thoughts with the rest of the group, specifically focusing on the last question.

SAY: History has shown that no matter who is in charge or what form of government a country has, the ruling authority dramatically affects how the citizens understand their lives and their roles in the world.

But what about the kingdom of God? There has never been any uncertainty regarding the concept of authority in God's kingdom. In both the Old and New Testaments, it is clear that God's "government" is based on the concept of a king—it is the unchallenged monarchy of God. And if you are a Christian, then you are a citizen of God's kingdom.

LEADER'S LOW-DOWN:

Dig In: The Devoted Warrior is an in-depth discipleship experience that is geared primarily toward Christian teens. However, you are likely to face teens you do not know personally or at least those whose faith journeys you haven't yet learned about. Because this is a discipleship experience, you *don't* want to dilute the message for the sake of nonbelievers, yet you *do* want to be sensitive to those who do not yet know Jesus personally.

We encourage you to be up-front from the start. Explain that *Dig In* is designed to bring Christians closer to Jesus and that you will be teaching as though everyone in the room has a personal relationship with Him. If they do not know Jesus or do not understand what this "Jesus stuff" is all about, they are invited to stay and learn what it looks like to be a follower of Christ. They are welcome to write down any questions that cross their minds throughout the sessions (these can be recorded on the Notes pages at the back of their Training Manuals). Be sure to follow up with these particular youth after *Dig In*.

In everything you say and do, make an effort to include every teen. No matter where students are in their own faith walks, your attitude (oftentimes even more than your words) will impact their idea of how Jesus feels about them.

There is a big difference between a kingdom and a democracy. Living in a democracy is a great thing, but it can also hurt our spiritual lives if we allow it to affect the way we think about God. After all, we're used to the idea that if we don't like something a leader does, we vote him out. If we don't like a law, we vote to change it. But citizens in a monarchy don't argue with or vote against the king. They know that the king is in charge, and that's that.

The kingdom of God is *not* a democracy. If we don't like one of God's commands, we don't just "vote" against it. If we don't like God's answer to a prayer, we don't vote him out of office! We're citizens in a kingdom and we honor our King, no matter what. We respect our King, we obey our King, and we fight for our King, regardless of the cost. As citizens of the kingdom, there is one truth that is central in our lives: the King is in charge!

So if *we* know that we're citizens in a *kingdom*, the important question that confronts us is very simple: What does this *mean* for us? How should it change the way we think? the way we live? What does it mean for our purpose, our life, and our loyalty? What should be changed in us when we view ourselves as the people of an all-knowing, almighty King?

"LORD" ISN'T JUST A NICKNAME

SAY: Let's dive a little deeper into this idea by looking at another word in the Bible that's used to describe Jesus.

Invite a volunteer to read aloud Romans 10:9.

SAY: We call Jesus "Lord" because He is God. We call Him "Lord" because He has all the power of the universe at His command. We call Jesus "Lord" because He came to earth as a human being with one purpose in mind: saving us from sin and death. We call Jesus "Lord" because He suffered brutal torture and death on our behalf, dying on the cross in our place. We call

Jesus "Lord" because He rose from the dead, defeating sin and opening the way for us to spend eternity in heaven with Him. We call Him "Lord" because He ascended to heaven and reigns in power. We call Him "Lord" because He's coming back some day. Jesus is worthy of our worship—He is worthy of being called "Lord."

But what exactly does the word *lord* mean? Is it just a religious word? Is it simply a title for God? Or does it mean something more? This may come as a surprise to some of you, but the word *lord* is *not* just a nickname for Jesus—it's central to our understanding of what it means to be a Christian.

Turn to pages four and five in your Training Manual, and get back together with your constitution-writing group. Read the description of the word *lord* together, then talk about the discussion questions.

After 10 to 15 minutes, gather everyone back together.

ASK: What stands out to you from your group's discussion? Based on what you talked about, what does it really mean to confess that "Jesus is Lord" as it says in Romans 10:9?

SAY: When we declare that Jesus is our Lord—when we recognize that He is the King of our lives—we become citizens of His kingdom. But we're not called to simply exist and hang out in the kingdom. All citizens have a job to do.

In fact, if we were just called to hang out in the kingdom, we could end up like those in the "Spineless Kingdom."

Play DVD clip "Spineless Kingdom" (Length 4:12)

SHORT SYNOPSIS:
"Spineless Kingdom"

This clip uses a mock nature show called *Unbridled Universe* to show what the human species would become without a sense of right and wrong.

This clip is a bit of an exaggeration—but really, to be a citizen in God's kingdom, we must stand up for what's right. We've got to have backbone.

Did you know that in the country of Israel today, every citizen—both men and women—and all resident aliens are *required* to join the military at the age of 18? That's right, *all* citizens automatically become soldiers for their country. It's the same with God's kingdom. You're called not just to citizenship—you're called to be a soldier in God's army, to fight courageously for Him. This isn't a volunteer army, where you can choose either to be a soldier or to sit on the sidelines. You're automatically called to be a warrior.

When we name Jesus as our King, we swear an oath of allegiance to Him. We give Him everything. We give Him all of us.

SWEARING THE OATH

Show students the movie clip you prepared from *The Lord of the Rings: The Return of the King* Extended Version. The clip begins at 1:19:55 (based on 0:00:00 at start of studio credits) when Peregrin is sitting on a bench and he says to himself, "What were you thinking, Peregrin Took..." The clip ends at approximately 1:22:10 when the Steward of Gondor sits down on his throne after saying, "Disloyalty with vengeance."

LEADER'S LOW-DOWN:

Though copyright law is somewhat vague when it comes to using short clips of films for Christian education purposes, we recommend that you play it safe by checking to see if your church has an umbrella license (see the Motion Picture Licensing Corporation's web site, www.mplc.com, for more information) or by seeking permission from the film's production company to show this clip.

In this clip, the small hobbit Peregrin Took pledges an oath of fealty to the Steward of Gondor. He commits to fight as a soldier in his army and to do his bidding.

After the clip, **SAY: Peregrin pledged his life to Gondor—his obedience, his loyalty, his devotion. He made the Steward of Gondor his lord and his king. He swore to fight for him, to the death if needed.**

In our country, we don't make oaths to a king, but when people choose to become citizens of America, they do have to swear an oath.

Invite everyone to turn to page six of their Training Manuals and have a volunteer read aloud the United States Naturalization Oath while everyone else reads along.

Here's the text of the oath for your convenience:

"I hereby declare, on oath, that I absolutely and entirely renounce and abjure all allegiance and fidelity to any foreign prince, potentate, state or sovereignty of whom or which I have heretofore been a subject or citizen; that I will support and defend the Constitution and laws of the United States of America against all enemies, foreign and domestic; that I will bear true faith and allegiance to the same; that I will bear arms on behalf of the United States when required by the law; that I will perform noncombatant service in the Armed Forces of the United States when required by the law; that I will perform work of national importance under civilian direction when required by the law; and that I take this obligation freely without any mental reservation or purpose of evasion; so help me God."[1]

SAY: This is what it means to be a citizen of our country. But what would it be like to swear an oath to our King, Jesus? It means we renounce all other allegiances—to the world, to our friends, to our dreams—they all become secondary to our allegiance to Jesus. It means we swear to defend our kingdom against all enemies, no matter the cost. It means we're committed to serve and obey our King, doing whatever He calls us to. It means we will do any work God calls us to. It means we commit to God freely and without doubts holding us back.

As warriors for our King, we are to live in strength and courage. We are to live as followers of Jesus. Do you realize that in Scripture Jesus never invited people to "become Christians"? Jesus asked people to *follow* Him—He used this phrase 32 times in the Bible. The question we each need to respond to isn't "Are you a Christian?"—it's "are you a *follower* of Christ?" Or let me put it another way: The question isn't "Do you believe Jesus is God?"—the question is, "Is Jesus your *Lord*?"

When Jesus commanded His disciples, "follow Me," it didn't just mean "come along for the ride." It meant that the lives of the 12 disciples would be radically changed. It meant they'd now enter a battlefield, full of suffering and danger.

For the disciples, "follow Me" meant homelessness.

Have a volunteer read aloud Matthew 8:20.

SAY: For the disciples, "follow Me" meant public humiliation, mockery, and persecution.

Have a volunteer read aloud Matthew 10:17–23.

SAY: For the disciples, "follow Me" meant the possibility of death.

Have a volunteer read aloud Matthew 10:38–39.

SAY: Today our decision to be followers of Jesus isn't any less dramatic. To be a warrior for our King means we lose things in this world. "Follow Me" *still means* we may have to give up the comforts of our home. It still means we may face humiliation, mockery, or persecution. And in the world today, for many followers of Jesus, it still means death.

MODERN WARRIORS

SAY: Matthew 11:12 gives us insight into what it's like to be a part of God's Kingdom. The English Standard Version translates it this way: "From the days of John the Baptist until now the kingdom of heaven has suffered violence, and the violent take it by force." As citizens of God's kingdom, we face violent resistance. How do we respond to it? Do we shrink back in fear when we're faced with persecution or worldly shame? Do we hide our faith in order to avoid uncomfortable situations? Do we give Jesus lip service without totally living like He is our Lord and our King?

Get back together with your small group of three to five one more time to talk about some questions. You'll find them on page seven in your Training Manual.

After about 15 minutes, have everyone gather back together and **SAY:** Let me tell you the story of an unlikely warrior. Thomas—who was also called Didymus—was one of Jesus' disciples. Yet he didn't always come across as the most enthusiastic follower. At times he was sarcastic, at other times he was a critic. His claim to fame, though, was his penchant for doubting. He is often called "Doubting Thomas" because he couldn't believe that Jesus rose from the dead. In fact, he told the other disciples, "Unless I see the nail marks in his hands and put my finger where the nails were, and put my hand into his side, I will not believe it" (John 20:25). His doubts were perhaps a lot like what you might experience—it's just human to doubt, to have questions, to be afraid.

LEADER'S LOW-DOWN:

Christian teens who have heard the same Bible stories over and over again can become jaded, feeling like they've "heard it all before." You can play a critical role in helping teens overcome this mind-set by bringing Bible stories to life through your tone of voice. As you tell the story of Thomas, use an animated tone and sincere facial expressions to help students see Thomas as more than a character in a story. Show them the real Thomas—a person just like them, faced with the same dramatic choice confronting them: naming Jesus as Lord!

But that's not the end of Thomas' story. A week later, the resurrected Jesus appeared to Thomas and let him touch the nail marks and the spear wound in His side. And Thomas responded with the most simple—yet utterly profound—declaration of allegiance to Jesus. He cried out, "My Lord and my God!" (John 20:28).

And when Thomas called Jesus his Lord, he meant it. Church history records that Thomas dedicated his life to telling others about Jesus by traveling as a missionary to Persia, Parthia, and India. While in India, Thomas was attacked and tortured. This man who once had a shaky faith died as a gallant warrior, first being run through with spears and then being burned to death in an oven. [2]

We can respond to Jesus just as the warrior-disciple Thomas did. Instead of living as lukewarm, cultural Christians, we can call Jesus "My Lord and My God!" *And we can truly mean it.* We can live in total, utter devotion to Jesus as our Lord, our Master, and our King.

Short SYNOPSIS: "Invisible Battle"

In this clip, a teenager sees glimpses of the spiritual battle that is raging for his generation. God uses these visions to inspire him to become a warrior for Christ right in his own high school.

Is God speaking to you? Is He calling you to be a modern-day warrior? Let's see how God spoke to a teenager who became a warrior right in his own high school.

Play DVD clip "Invisible Battle" (Length 4:41)

MINISTRY TIME

SAY: Just as the hobbit Peregrin knelt before the Steward of Gondor in the clip we watched, let's kneel before Jesus as a sign of our commitment to live as warriors for our King.

LEADER'S LOW-DOWN:

When students are praying, join in by silently praying *for* them. If your group is small enough, pray for each student by name during this time—asking God to work powerfully in their lives during this *Dig In* experience. Pray that throughout these sessions, teenagers will commit to live lives fully dedicated to Jesus!

Play quiet music in the background and invite students to kneel around the wooden cross you set up before the session. Invite them to quietly pray, swearing the oath that Thomas swore to Jesus: "My Lord and My God!" Encourage students to pray and quietly worship for about 10 minutes. Conclude their prayer time by praying:

We love you, Jesus. You are our Lord, our Master, our God, our King. Help us to live in complete devotion to You. In Jesus' name, amen.

MAKE IT REAL

Have everyone gather back together, standing. Prompt them to turn to page eight in their Training Manuals.

SAY: Over 150 years ago someone wrote lyrics that meet us right where we are today. This song, "Onward, Christian Soldiers," speaks to the battle we all have to fight, united in our devotion to Jesus our King. Let's finish by reading it aloud together responsively—just follow the directions on the left side which say who is to read what. As you read and listen, think about the meaning of the words.

LEADER'S LOW-DOWN:

If your group isn't used to reading aloud together, some students might be timid or quiet. Counteract this by setting the tone right away—read loudly, with energy, and with triumph! Express the amazing commitment and victory of the words through the emotional tone in your voice. Teens will quickly catch on to the passion you communicate and will join in, speaking in strength and victory!

On the next page is a copy of the Responsive Reading from page eight of the Training Manual:

ONWARD, CHRISTIAN SOLDIERS[3]

by Sabine Baring-Gould

ALL:
Onward, Christian soldiers, marching as to war,
With the cross of Jesus going on before!
Christ, the royal Master, leads against the foe;
Forward into battle see his banner go!

GIRLS:
At the sign of triumph Satan's host doth flee;
On then, Christian soldiers, on to victory!

GUYS:
Hell's foundations quiver at the shout of praise;
Brothers, lift your voices, loud your anthems raise!

ALL:
Like a mighty army moves the Church of God;
Brothers, we are treading where the saints have trod.

GIRLS:
We are not divided, all one body we:
One in hope and doctrine, one in charity.

GUYS:
Crowns and thrones may perish, kingdoms rise and wane,
But the Church of Jesus constant will remain.

ALL:
Gates of hell can never against that Church prevail;
We have Christ's own promise, and that cannot fail.

TRUE POWER, TOTAL AUTHORITY

WHAT'S THE POINT?

We live in obedient devotion to Jesus because He is the ultimate authority over the universe—and over our everyday lives.

A QUICK GLANCE...

MINUTES	SECTION	SUPPLIES
up to 30	Optional Warm-Up Activity	Blue index cards, white index cards, pink index cards, pens, several rolls of masking tape
10 to 15	Matching Mottoes	Training Manuals, pens
25 to 30	Words to Live By	Bibles, paper, pens
20 to 25	Molded Hearts, Shaped Lives	Training Manuals, Bibles, several video game controllers, several dog leashes and collars, a quantity of clay or play dough, a cross up front
up to 10	True Power, Total Authority	Bibles, Dig In DVD, TV, DVD player
up to 10	Ministry Time	Training Manuals, pens, worship CD and CD player or a musician
up to 10	Make It Real	Training Manuals, pens

Before the event begins, make sure every teenager has his or her Training Manual. Set up your large, free-standing wooden cross near the front of your meeting area and ready a CD player with worshipful, instrumental music. Set up a TV and DVD player and be ready to play the *Dig In* DVD. Gather blue, white, and pink index cards—you'll need enough so that every student can get one of each color. Also get a hold of several video game controllers, dog leashes and collars, and lumps of clay. These will be used as object lessons, and you'll need one of each item for every five or six students, plus enough clay or play dough for each teen to have a piece.

OPTIONAL WARM-UP ACTIVITY

Welcome teenagers as they arrive and start out with a fun game. Give each student a pen, a blue index card, a white index card, and a pink index card. Ask them to spread out around the room and privately write their answers to these questions.

SAY: On the blue card, I'd like you to anonymously write your answer to this question: What is your favorite TV show?

Allow students time to write, then **SAY:**
Now on the white card, write one word that describes your personality.

When they're done writing, **SAY:**
Last, on the pink card, write your answer to this question: When you think about your life as an adult, what is your dream job?

LEADER'S LOW-DOWN:

If you can't get a hold of blue, white, and pink index cards, you can use any color combination you'd like.

When students have written all their answers, collect all the cards. Divide them into three piles (by color) and shuffle each pile. Then redistribute the cards so that each teenager gets a new blue, white, and pink card. Pass around several rolls of masking tape so that each student can tear off three pieces.

SAY: Your job now is to try to match each of your cards with the person you think they describe. You can wander around the room and mingle with each other. When you think you've identified someone who fits one of your cards, tape it to the person's back. You can't *ask* them if you guessed right—and they can't check what's on the card.

But here's the catch: Each person can only have one card of each color taped to his/her back. If you think someone wrote the answer on your white card, but you see that they already have a white card taped to their back, then you can't pick that person— you'll have to guess someone else. Make sense?

When everyone understands the basic idea of the game, let them get started mingling and affixing cards. The game ends when everyone has a blue, white, and pink card taped to their back.

When the game is over, have everyone remove the cards from their backs and see if anyone guessed right.

ASK: How well did people match cards to you?
Are you surprised by any of the guesses? If so, how?
How easy was it to guess what other people wrote?

LEADER'S LOW-DOWN:

If you have time, you can add an extra round of fun to the game. When everyone has removed and read the cards from their backs, have them each determine if anyone matched cards correctly to them. If any of the cards were right, have those students stick them on their backs. Explain that students should then grab the cards that were incorrectly affixed to them and should take a few minutes to mingle again and see if they can guess the right person to match the cards. This extra round of matching will increase the chances of cards being matched to people correctly.

After the game, have everyone grab a Training Manual, a pen, and take a seat. (Have students create rows with their chairs, facing the front of the room.)

MATCHING MOTTOES

SAY: We've just tried to match dreams and ideas to each other. Now we'll try another type of matching. Form groups of three with people sitting near you and turn to page nine in your Training Manual. You've got five minutes to work together to try to match the cities to their mottoes.

After five minutes, read the answers to the group:

CITY	MOTTO
Anchorage, Alaska	City of Lights
Atlanta, Georgia	The World's Next Great International City
Baltimore, Maryland	The City that Reads
Boston, Massachusetts	Beantown
Chicago, Illinois	The Windy City
Denver, Colorado	The Mile High City
Houston, Texas	The Space City
Indianapolis, Indiana	The Circle City
Las Vegas, Nevada	The Entertainment Capital of the World
Los Angeles, California	City of the Angels
Miami, Florida	Gateway to the Americas
Milwaukee, Wisconsin	The Cream City
Minneapolis, Minnesota	City of Lakes
Nashville, Tennessee	The Music City
Philadelphia, Pennsylvania	The City of Brotherly Love
Portland, Oregon	The City of Roses
Roswell, New Mexico	The Aliens Aren't the Only Reason to Visit!
San Francisco, California	The City by the Bay
Seattle, Washington	The Emerald City[4]

After teenagers have heard all the right answers, **ASK:**
- **How were you able to guess the ones you got right?**
- **Now that you know the answers to the others, do they make sense to you?**
- **Which city mottoes are the most obvious matches?**
- **Which seemed the least obvious to you?**

SAY: Webster's Dictionary defines a motto as "a word, phrase, or sentence chosen as expressive of the goals or ideals of a nation, a group, etc." Mottoes are meant to express an essential trait. This is why national, state, or city mottoes are often posted at the boundary line to welcome people as they enter. The motto communicates the vision and identity of that place.

When you think about what it means to be a Christian, what are the goals, ideals, and essential traits of your faith? What is the vision or identity at the heart of being a Christian? Get back together in your group of three and work together to come up with a one-sentence motto that describes what it means to be a Christian.

After a few minutes, **ASK:**
So what did you come up with?

Affirm trios as they share their ideas, commenting on the strengths of each motto that is shared.

Then **ASK:** Was it hard to boil down the essential traits of Christianity into just a few words? Why or why not?

WORDS TO LIVE BY. . .

SAY: In the Old Testament God gave His people a sort of motto. But instead of posting it at the city limits, it was posted on the gates, doorways, and even on their hands and foreheads. Let's read it.

Invite a volunteer to read aloud Deuteronomy 6:4–9 while everyone else reads along in their own Bibles.

SAY: This statement, "The Lord our God, the Lord is one. Love the Lord your God with all your heart and with all your soul and with all your strength," is called the *Shema*. And we can see one idea really clearly in the passage we just read: that God is saying,

"Whatever you do, *don't forget this.*" The ideas are so essential to God's people that they are to teach them to their children and literally post them all over the place so that they are constantly reminded of them.

Why is this motto so important? First, it established that the Jewish people worshiped a totally unique God: the one true sovereign Lord. This in and of itself set the Jewish people apart from their neighboring countries, and all the world. The *Shema* goes on to emphasize that they are never to lose their love for God, and never quit loving Him with all their being. Look back at verse 5—do you notice how no part of the human is left out? The heart—which in Hebrew includes the mind and its faculties—and the soul encompass the entire person. This includes our will, our reason, and our passions. And on top of this, we are to love Jesus with all our might, with all our strength, with everything!

This motto, in essence, is a statement of utter, complete, total, absolute devotion to God. It established the identity of God's people, setting them apart from all the other people on the earth. It was the foundation for their goals. Their devotion was their distinguishing characteristic.

In Mark 12:28, we read that one of the teachers of the law came to Jesus and asked him, "Of all the commandments, which is the most important?" Jesus does not hesitate. He states, "Hear, O Israel: The Lord our God, the Lord is one. Love the Lord your God with all your heart and with all your soul and with all your mind and with all your strength" (Mark 12:29-30). In fact, in Matthew 22:40, Jesus explains that all laws in the Old Testament and all the teachings of the prophets are summed up in these words and in the Christian's love for his or her neighbor.

"Love the Lord your God with all your heart and with all your soul and with all your mind and with all your strength." *This* is the motto of the Christian.

But what does this motto really mean? Let's form new small groups of five or six people to explore the *Shema* together.

Pass out paper and pens to each group and ask someone in each group to write this phrase at the top of each paper:

What does it mean to love the Lord your God with all your heart and with all your soul and with all your mind and with all your strength and with all your_____?

SAY: I'm going to name a word. Once I say it, I want you to mentally plug it into the blank on the top of your paper. What would it mean to love God in this way? Talk in your group and list on your paper words, ideas, or phrases that explain what you think it means or what it would look like for a Christian to love God in this way. You'll have just two minutes to brainstorm and write answers, then I'll shout out a new word for you to plug into the blank and discuss. Got it?

When everyone understands how the exercise will work, **SAY** the first word: **Time.**

Every two minutes, name a new word from this list:
   Money
   Schoolwork
   Family relationships
   Hobbies
   Friend relationships
   Dreams
   Dating relationships
   Life

LEADER'S LOW-DOWN:

Encourage students to be creative and specific as they brainstorm the implications of each word and what it means to love God fully in that area. Suggest that they consider what a person might have to give up in order to love God in that way. Prompt them to describe specific actions that exemplify total dedication to God in that area.

When students are done writing their ideas regarding "life," **ASK:**
What were some of the common themes in your discussion?
Which ideas rose to the top as the most important?
What does it look like for someone to love God with all of her being?

SAY: When we talk about loving God with all of us—with every part of our life, our future, our dreams—we're not just talking about an emotion. Love in this verse isn't a mushy feeling—it's something different. It's devotion demonstrated through action. Loving God with our entire being means surrendering every aspect of our lives to Him and obeying Him in all things.

MOLDED HEARTS, SHAPED LIVES

SAY: In Scripture, loving God is directly linked with obedience. Look at Deuteronomy 11:13 and Joshua 22:5.

Invite volunteers to read Deuteronomy 11:13 and Joshua 22:5 aloud while everyone else follows along in their own Bibles.

SAY: These Old Testament passages show that love and obedience are totally connected. But perhaps it is most powerfully displayed in Jesus' teaching to His disciples in John 14:15–24.

Have volunteers read aloud John 14:15–24 while everyone else reads along, then **ASK** the group:
What stands out to you from this passage?
Is it possible to love Jesus without obeying Him?
Why is obedience such an important part of love?

SAY: Loving Jesus with our hearts, our minds, our souls, and with all our strength starts with total obedience. A. W. Tozer was right on when he wrote, "Full lordship demands complete submission." What he is saying is that there is no limit to this sort of obedience. If Jesus is your King and Lord, then you are willing to obey Him completely in every single aspect of your life. Throughout history, kings have demanded obedience from their subjects. Their reign was finite—they didn't live forever. And so the obedience of their subjects was finite—it ended when that particular king died. But Christ commands a different sort of obedience because He is a different sort of King. His reign, authority, and command are infinite. And so our obedience is likewise infinite and eternal. It knows no bounds!

LEADER'S LOW-DOWN:

You may want to refer students to the section on the meaning of *Lord* and *Lordship* from Session One on page four in their Training Manuals.

SAY: Now it's one thing to *talk* about obedience, but it is another thing to actually do it. Our society isn't really big on the idea of obeying someone else. We like to think, "I'm my own person—I can do what I want!" The world sees obedience as a negative thing, and it's easy to let that mind-set creep into our own perspectives.

Hold up the dog leash and collar.

SAY: Some people think of obedience to God's rules like a chain around our neck holding us back from doing what we really want to do. They see obedience as something forced upon us, like God is reining us in. They view obedience as a leash upon our lives, keeping us from our real desires and preventing us from experiencing "the good life."

But you know what? They're wrong. In obeying God we find true *freedom*, not limitations.

Hold up the video game controller.

SAY: Other people think of obedience this way, like we're little video game characters and God is holding the controls, telling us exactly what to do and say, controlling every movement.

But guess what—they're wrong. God did not create us to be robots. God doesn't force us to do this or say that. He's given us free will and the opportunity to *choose* to obey Him. We obey Him not because we're forced to, but because we want to! We obey God because we love God.

Hold up a clump of clay or play dough so everyone can see it, then mold into a heart shape as you talk.

SAY: *This* is the right way to think of obedience. Obedience means saying to God, "Here I am. Use me. Mold me. Change me. Shape every part of me." It means we allow our actions, our attitudes—our whole lives—to be shaped by God. Isaiah 64:8 puts it this way: "O Lord, you are our Father. We are the clay, you are the potter; we are all the work of your hand." Obedience is a mindset of submission and surrender. It's a constant sense that we want God to shape us and change us according to His will.

We aren't *made* to obey God like a dog on a leash. We aren't *forced* to obey God like a video game character.

(Hold up the clay heart.)

Our obedience comes from a willing and ready heart.

Invite students to get back in their small groups of five or six (from the *Shema* brainstorming activity). Give each group a leash and collar, a video game controller, and a large lump of clay or play dough. Invite groups to turn to page 10 in their Training Manuals and follow the instructions there to guide their discussion. Allow about 10 minutes for groups to talk through the questions.

LEADER'S LOW-DOWN:

If you can't get enough video game controllers, you could also have kids use TV or VCR remote controls for this object lesson. Remote controls communicate the same idea of a machine responding to electronic commands, symbolizing the incorrect idea that God controls people through "forced" obedience.

During their discussion, small groups will talk about the meaning of the various object lessons. To conclude, each teen will create a clay symbol of obedience and lay it at the foot of the cross.

When all the students have set their clay creations at the foot of the cross, collect the dog leashes and video game controllers.

TRUE POWER, TOTAL AUTHORITY

SAY: Why should you obey Jesus? Not because your parents tell you to. Not because I tell you to. You should obey Jesus for one simple reason: because He is God! He has power over all the universe. He has total authority over all things, including us. Let's look at some Scriptures that explore this idea.

Invite a volunteer to read aloud Colossians 1:16–20 while everyone else reads along in their own Bibles.

ASK: What words or phrases in this passage point to Jesus' authority? What do they mean?

SAY: This passage pretty much covers it, doesn't it? Jesus has the power of creation—He made the world! Jesus has authority over all the powers, rulers, and authorities on this planet. Jesus has the power to hold everything in the universe together. Jesus is the authority—the head—over His church. He has the power to resurrect from the dead. He is supreme over all things. He is God! And through Jesus' death, Jesus had the authority to overcome the power of sin! Jesus has the *right* to be the authority in our lives. Let's hear it in His own words.

Invite a volunteer to read aloud Matthew 28:16–20.

SAY: Jesus has all the authority on heaven and earth. He is *worthy* of our total devotion and obedience. We are to be totally committed to Him in everything we say and do. Just like soldiers obey orders, we follow Jesus' commands simply because He is our commanding officer. And in this passage, we see an image of what that obedience looks like. Jesus sends His followers out into the world so that we can be His witnesses. As soldiers, He has given us marching orders and a mission to fulfill for Him!

LEADER'S LOW-DOWN:

If you have time, you can expand this part of the session by asking teenagers to brainstorm and name some of Jesus' other commands. What actions might He have been referring to when He said, "If you love me, you'll keep my commandments?" Invite teenagers to flip through the Gospels in their Bibles to get ideas.

When we obey the Commander, He *will* use us and amaze us. We're going to watch a DVD clip and see how God used a teenager named Josh when he chose obedience.

Play DVD clip "Josh Webb" (Length 1:35)

SHORT SYNOPSIS:

"Josh Webb"
Sixteen-year-old Josh Webb shares how God used him to lead a youth rally. This clip will challenge your teens to lead NOW; they don't have to wait until they're older to be leaders.

MINISTRY TIME

SAY: I don't know about you, but this idea of total, utter, complete devotion and obedience is convicting. We all have areas of our lives where we fall short of this goal. We all need to make the motto of loving God with our whole beings more true in our daily lives. Let's take some time to pray individually about how we want to grow in these areas.

Grab your Training Manual and turn to page 11. Use the prompts to journal a prayer, asking God to show you areas in which you need to be more devoted to Him and asking Him for the strength to change through the power of the Holy Spirit.

Play worship music quietly in the background while students spread out around the room to journal their prayers. Allow about 10 minutes for students to pray, then invite everyone to return to their seats.

MAKE IT REAL

SAY: Now that we've talked to God about our need to be more fully devoted and obedient to Him, let's take it one step further. Let's talk to *each other*. When we share our spiritual growth commitments with another Christian, we can find encouragement and accountability as we put our commitments into action.

Find a partner and take some time to share with each other one area in your life in which you know you need to recognize Jesus' authority by obeying Him. Tell your partner what you'll commit to do as an act of obedience in that specific situation. I'd like each of you to write down your commitment as well as your partner's commitment in the Notes section at the back of your Training Manual. That way you can take your commitment seriously, and you can also encourage your partner to do the same.

Once you've written the two commitments, spend some time praying for each other and praising Jesus for His authority in your life.

LEADER'S LOW-DOWN

You may want to ask pairs to go even further in their encouragement of each other by having them exchange phone numbers or email addresses and commit to check in with each other during the week to see if they followed through on their spiritual growth commitments. At http://downloads.battlecry.com, you can download accountability partner business cards that your teens can fill out and exchange with their partners.

Allow students time to talk and pray, then close the session by praying something like:

Lord Jesus, all authority in heaven and on earth has been given to You. We praise You! We love You! We seek to obey You. We want to love You fully with every single aspect of our lives. Help us, Lord, to live in complete devotion and obedience to You. In Jesus' name, amen.

LEADER'S LOW-DOWN:

After this session, be sure to remove the clay symbols students placed at the foot of the cross.

SESSION THREE: I'M YOURS FOREVER!

WHAT'S THE POINT?

We respond to Jesus' death by totally committing our lives to Him and being willing to take up our own crosses.

A QUICK GLANCE...

MINUTES	SECTION	SUPPLIES
up to 30	Optional Warm-up Activity	Large paper bags, pens, Symbol Scavenger Hunt sheets, (Optional: various objects (see Leader's Low-Down box on page 47))
20 to 25	The Most Sacred of Symbols	Training Manuals, Bibles, pens, images of corporate logos (see top of page 46), (Optional: computer with PowerPoint, screen, projector)
10 to 15	I am Your Man Forever!	The Count of Monte Cristo DVD, DVD player, TV
10 to 15	Four Fatal Words	Bibles, Dig In DVD, TV, DVD player,
25 to 30	The Crux of the Matter	Bibles
15 to 20	Ministry Time	Bibles, Training Manuals, paper, pens
up to 15	Make It Real	Large wooden cross, nails, hammers, CD player and a worship CD or a musician

Before the event begins, make sure all your teenagers have their Training Manuals. Make copies (one for each pair of teens) of the "Symbol Scavenger Hunt" handout found on page 60. (Copying privileges are granted for page 60 only.) You can also download this handout free of charge at http://downloads.battlecry.com.

Set up a TV and DVD player and be ready to play the *Dig In* DVD.

You'll also need about five famous corporate logos. The best way to get these is to go on the Internet and copy the images from company web sites, then paste them onto PowerPoint slides. You can then project the images onto a screen for "The Most Sacred of Symbols" activity. Or, if you want to do it without technology, simply tear out logos from magazine ads or from printed materials like paper cups or, if you're artistic, draw the logos on pieces of paper. You'll want logos for companies like McDonald's, Starbucks, Nike, etc.

In addition, set up a TV and DVD player and cue up *The Count of Monte Cristo* to approximately 01:01:20 (based on 0:00:00 at the start of studio credits) when Edmond Dantes is running on the beach after he has escaped from prison. This clip is found in chapter 15 of most DVDs.

Set up the large, free-standing wooden cross near the front of your meeting area and ready a CD player with worshipful, instrumental music. Collect hammers and nails; you'll need one nail for each student.

OPTIONAL WARM-UP ACTIVITY

Welcome teenagers as they arrive and have them form pairs.

SAY: Today we're going on a Symbol Scavenger Hunt. During this scavenger hunt, you need to stay with your partner the entire time. In pairs, you'll have just 15 minutes to run around our building trying to find things that you think can be good symbols to represent what certain ideas mean to you. So, for example, if I said that you needed to find a symbol representing "family," you might grab some toy people from the church nursery, you might take the family picture out of your wallet, or you might pick a piece of jewelry you're wearing that someone in your family gave you. Be creative! You can pick anything at all that you think symbolizes the idea.

If the objects you find are small, I want you to pick them up and put them in a bag. You'll need to bring them back to the room with you. But if an object is too big to carry, you'll just write down what it is and where you found it.

Does everyone understand so far?

LEADER'S LOW-DOWN:

If you're meeting in a church building or retreat center, there likely will be lots of small objects students can find inside or outside, such as toys from children's Sunday school rooms, items from their backpacks or purses, objects from nature (if the weather permits that they go outside), clothes they are wearing, or stuff from their own suitcases if you're on a weekend retreat. However, if you're in an area that you think might not supply enough creative or symbolic objects, bring some yourself and set them up around the building ahead of time. You might want to bring items such as: books, toys and trinkets, sports equipment, magazines, pictures, kitchen gadgets, office supplies, stuffed animals…anything kids can get creative with!

Pass out pens, large paper bags, and the "Symbol Scavenger Hunt" hand-outs, one to each pair, and invite students to review the list of symbols they need to find.

SAY: Each time you pick an object to bring back, make sure you write down where you found it because you'll need to return it later. Now, look at your watches. You've got just 15 minutes to find symbols for all of these ideas, then I want to see all of you back in this room. You must be back in 15 minutes even if you don't have all the objects you want. Got it? OK, ready? Go!

LEADER'S LOW-DOWN:

Depending on where you're meeting, you may need to lay down some ground rules, such as identifying areas where students *can* go and where they *can't*. Also, if you're on a retreat and students have suitcases or bags of their own items, be sure to clarify that teenagers *cannot* look through each other's stuff and take items from other people's bags. If they're going to get stuff from their rooms, clarify that they can only collect objects from their own bags.

After 15 minutes when everyone has returned with their objects and lists, instruct pairs to "pair up," forming new groups of four.

SAY: OK, now it's show and tell time! In your groups, I'd like you to go through your lists together, each time sharing with each other which object your team selected as a symbol and what it means to you. If you don't actually have one of the objects with you, describe in detail what it looks like. Do your best to explain *why* each object symbolizes each idea to you and your partner.

LEADER'S LOW-DOWN:

The process of explaining symbols to each other will help teenagers get to know each other on a much deeper level than just talking about likes and dislikes or hobbies. Suddenly they'll be sharing truths about their values in a deep way…and it's fun too! Use variations of this game in the future in your youth group to help students continue to intensify their relationships. One easy five-minute version of this game is simply to say: **Select an object that you're wearing, or that's in your purse or backpack, that best represents…** (name an idea). Kids will have to scramble to come up with creative interpretations—especially if they don't have any trinkets with them! But you'll be amazed at the symbolic meanings they can find in tennis shoes, a favorite T-shirt, or a comfy pair of jeans!

After everyone has returned their objects, have everybody grab a Training Manual and a chair and take a seat. (Have students create rows with their chairs, facing the front of the room.)

THE MOST SACRED OF SYMBOLS

SAY: You were really creative in your use of symbols. Symbols are images or objects that represent an idea. I'm going to show you some images, and then I want you to tell me what they represent.

Show students the corporate logos you collected, either via PowerPoint or holding up the images. After each image, **ASK** the group:

What do you think of when you see this image?
Does this image define the idea it is representing? If so, how?
What does the image communicate?

Once kids have discussed all the logos, point to the wooden cross at the front of the room.

SAY: The cross is the visual symbol of Christianity. It is the one image, above all others, that people associate with our faith.

As you point to the cross, ask the group:

What do you think of when you see this image?
Does *this* image define the idea it is representing? If so, how?
How has this image become devalued in today's culture? (i.e. worn by pop stars, fashion statement, good luck charm)
What are examples of times the cross has been misrepresented? (i.e. The Crusades, Nazi Germany, Ku Klux Klan)
How can we be good stewards of this symbol?

SAY: The cross represents Jesus' death on our behalf. Though we often think of the cross as a positive symbol, we also need to remember what it immediately meant to people during Jesus' time. It's a visual representation of crucifixion—a popular form of brutal public execution in the first century. Let's look a little more closely at what crucifixion was like.

Turn to page 12 in your Training Manual and take a moment to quietly read about what Jesus went through when He was crucified.

For your reference, here is the text students will be reading:

DEATH ON A CROSS

Before Jesus was crucified, He was beaten and whipped brutally. His back would have been severely bloodied after the whip tore through skin and mus-cle. Jesus was then nailed by each wrist to the cross. Then His feet were placed atop each other, and a large nail driven through the arch of each, affixing them to the cross.

Physician C. Truman Davis wrote a medical analysis of crucifixion called "The Crucifixion of Jesus." Here is how he described what Jesus went through next: "As Jesus slowly sagged down with more weight on the nails in the wrists, excruciating, fiery pain shot along the fingers and up the arms to explode in the brain . . . As He pushed Himself upward to avoid this stretching torment, He placed His full weight on the nail through His feet. Again there was searing agony as the nail tore through the nerves between the metatarsal bones of His feet. At this point, another phenomenon occurred. As the arms fatigued, great waves of cramps swept over the muscles, knotting them in deep relentless, throbbing pain. With these cramps came the inability to push Himself upward. Hanging by the arms, the pectoral muscles, the large muscles of the chest, were paralyzed and the intercostal muscles, the small muscles between the ribs, were unable to act. Air could be drawn into the lungs, but could not be exhaled. Jesus fought to raise Himself in order to get even one short breath. Finally, the carbon dioxide level increased in the lungs and in the blood stream, and the cramps partially subsided."[5]

Jesus' heart and lungs were weakened until he eventually died. After His death, He was pierced through with a spear.

When students are done reading, **SAY:**

This is the symbol we wear around our necks. _This_ is what the cross represents. _This_ is the terrible torture and pain Jesus went through for you and for me. We get so used to seeing the cross and to talking about Jesus' death, that sometimes it's good to get a shocking reminder like this one of what Jesus went through.

But _why_ did Jesus go through this agony? Why did He die? Let's look at Scripture to discover the purpose for all Jesus' endured.

Invite volunteers to read aloud the following passages:

John 3:16
Romans 3:22–26

Romans 5:6–11
Romans 6:23
Colossians 1:21–22

ASK: Based on these Scriptures, why did Jesus suffer and die? What did Jesus' death accomplish?

Summarize the basic points students share, being sure to emphasize that Jesus died because of His love for us and that His death paid the penalty for our sin and gives us the opportunity to be reconciled with God.

I AM YOUR MAN FOREVER!

SAY: How do we react to this amazing act of love? How do we respond to this life-saving sacrifice? Let's look at a movie clip and explore our response to what Jesus did for us.

LEADER'S LOW-DOWN:

Though copyright law is somewhat vague when it comes to using short clips of films for Christian education purposes, we recommend that you play it safe by checking to see if your church has an umbrella license (see the Motion Picture Licensing Corporation's web site www.mplc.com for more information) or by seeking permission from the film's production company to show this clip.

Show students the movie clip you prepared from *The Count of Monte Cristo* DVD. The clip begins at 01:01:20 (based on 0:00:00 at the start of studio credits) when Edmond Dantes is running on the beach after he has escaped from prison. This clip is found in chapter 15 of most DVDs. The clip ends at approximately 01:05:01 after Jacapo tells Dantes, "I am your man forever!"

LEADER'S LOW-DOWN:

In this scene, Edmond Dantes has been taken prisoner by some bandits. He is then forced by the bandits to fight another prisoner named Jacapo. They are to fight with knives to the death; whoever survives will join the crew of bandits. Edmond wins the fight, physically pinning Jacapo to the ground. But instead of cutting Jacapo's throat, Edmond plunges his knife into the sand and bargains with the bandits to save Jacapo's life. Jacapo responds gratefully, saying, "I am your man forever!"

After the clip, **SAY:**

Edmond saved Jacapo's life, and Jacapo responded like any of us would have, from the depth of his heart saying, "I am your man forever!"

Just like Jacapo, we were condemned to death. But through His own death on the cross, Jesus saved our lives! The only natural response is to say, like Jacapo, "I am your man forever!" or "I am your woman forever!"

Think of it this way: imagine a soldier in a combat zone. Bullets are whizzing by, grenades are exploding just feet away. The soldier has been severely wounded by a bullet in his leg—he can't walk. The enemy is moving in and the soldier's only means of escape appears to be cut off. He's trapped! To make matters worse, he's out of ammo. He knows his death is certain.

Suddenly he hears a sound on his right. He pivots and finds his commanding officer running to him, dodging bullets all the way. His commanding officer then pulls the soldier up by the arm, hoisting him over his shoulder. Defying all the odds, he runs backwards, shooting at the enemy as he makes his escape. Unbelievably, the soldier has been saved! He knows his commanding officer risked life and limb to save his life. How grateful do you think he'd be to his commanding officer? Wouldn't that soldier be devoted to the officer forever?

Now multiply that gratefulness by about a million. Jesus is our commanding officer and He stepped in to save us. But He didn't just save us from physical danger—Jesus saved us from sin, from death, from eternal separation from God in hell. C.T. Studd put it this way: "If Jesus Christ be God and died for me, then no sacrifice can be too great for me to make for Him." Our only proper response is to cry out to Jesus, "I am yours forever!"

FOUR FATAL WORDS

SAY: Let's look at someone who made that same sort of commitment to Jesus: Rachel.

Play DVD clip "Rachel" (Length 2:36)

Almost 2000 years before Rachel Scott made the ultimate sacrifice, another individual lived and died totally sold-out to Christ. His name was Peter.

SHORT SYNOPSIS: "Rachel"

In this powerful clip, Rachel Scott's friends and family tell her story. At age seventeen, Rachel lost her life in the Columbine school shootings for professing that she believed in God. Rachel planned on going on a Teen Mania mission trip, but her life was cut short before she had a chance.

Tradition tells us that Peter was martyred upside down on a cross during Nero's reign. But it was 35 years prior to his actual crucifixion that Peter made his decision to follow Christ's own manner of death. It all took place in Ceasarea Philippi at the base of the great Mt. Hermon, near the northernmost boundary of ancient Israel. He was about 25 miles north of his hometown on the northern shores of the Galilean Sea. There Peter uttered four words that would change the course of his life and eventually lead him all the way to that fateful day in Rome.

Pause, then **SAY:**

Keep this picture of Peter being crucified upside down on a cross in your head while we read a passage from Scripture. That image is, in essence, the definition of what it means to be a devoted disciple.

Invite a volunteer to read aloud Matthew 16:13–16 while everyone else reads along in their Bibles.

ASK: What were those four life-changing words?

SAY: Let's follow the progression of this pivotal passage. First Peter recognizes that Jesus is the Christ. Jesus affirms Peter's words and shares with His disciples that He must go to Jerusalem and be killed. Upon hearing this, Peter rebukes Jesus—for how could his King die? Jesus then corrects Peter and reaffirms His mission of death. But it is not until 16:24 that we learn how Jesus will die and the implications for everyone who confesses "You are the Christ." Not only does Jesus respond to the disciple, "Yes, Peter, I must go die on the cross," but He says something far more shocking. In essence, He says, "Peter, you must also go to the cross after Me . . . that is, if what you said was true." And that is the very essence of discipleship.

THE CRUX OF THE MATTER

Invite students to form small groups of three to five and to re-read Matthew 16:24. Ask groups the following discussion questions, allowing about two minutes for discussion after each question.

ASK: Why does Jesus say this?
What do you think this means, practically speaking?
Now that you know what dying on the cross was like, what do you think this statement meant to the disciples when they first heard it? What do you think they felt it meant?
How is the cross a symbol of what it means to be a disciple?
How does the cross define the Christian faith?

Have everyone gather back together, then **ASK:**

What stood out to you from your group's discussion?
Summarize what you think Matthew 16:24 means.

SAY: When the signers of the Declaration of Independence in 1776 penned their names to the scandalous document, they branded themselves as traitors. By asserting their autonomy from mother England, they were immediately considered enemies of the British. The British army was given orders to find them and kill them. When the founding fathers signed their names to the Declaration of Independence, they knew the risk. They knew that they were in essence signing their own death certificate.

Similarly, when we sign up to be a Christian—when we declare to Jesus, "You are the Christ! You are my Lord! You are my King!"—we're signing our own death certificate. We're saying, "I'm willing to deny myself—to die to my own dreams and desires—and to live only for Jesus."

Taking up our cross means death to self-centeredness, death to pride, death to sin's control in our lives. It might mean death to popularity and friendships. It might mean death to our own plans for our lives. It might even mean physical death—that's certainly what it meant to Peter.

Let's look at some passages that illustrate this idea beautifully.

Invite volunteers to read aloud the following passages:

Romans 6:11–13
Galatians 2:20
Galatians 6:14

SAY: When we die to ourselves, it means we don't let sin call the shots in our lives. We've crucified our own will and replaced it with Christ's. It means that we no longer live our lives based on what the world will think of us—we live totally focused on Jesus.

In church history, when men or women committed to become monks or nuns, they took vows, promising to live in poverty, chastity, and obedience. Their vows were a refusal to have any worldly attachments. They had a willingness to entirely give up the love of things, to surrender their sexuality to God, and to submit their will entirely to God.

ASK: Though vows like this are extreme, can you learn from them?
How could their example apply to Christian teenagers today?

SAY: "If any one would come after me, he must deny himself and take up his cross and follow me." This is the model of the Christian life. The only proper response to Jesus' death on the cross is a dramatic one, of the same caliber; we respond by being willing to go to the cross ourselves.

We're willing to surrender ourselves to Jesus because He surrendered *everything* on our behalf. Jesus' love, exhibited especially in His death, is what drives our total commitment to Him.

MINISTRY TIME

Invite teenagers to return to their small groups of three to five students. Pass out paper and a pen to each student. Then instruct small groups to read aloud the description of Jesus' death found in Matthew 26:62–68 and 27:27–50. Ask groups to discuss these questions:

How does reading about Jesus' death make you feel?
How do you want to respond?

When groups are done talking, ask students to find their own space in the room.

SAY: We each have our own thoughts and feelings when we consider how we'll respond to the cross. Let's consider together how one man, Isaac Watts, wrote about his own feelings and resolution when he thought about all Jesus did for him through His death on the cross. Turn to page 13 in your Training Manual and read it privately. Imagine you're standing before the cross, watching Jesus die for you. Write your response to the cross on your piece of paper. You can write whatever you want—a poem, a prayer, or even a list of commitments. Whatever you write is private—just between you and God.

For your reference, here is the text of the hymn:

ALAS! AND DID MY SAVIOR BLEED *by Isaac Watts*[6]
Alas! and did my Savior bleed
And did my sovereign die?
Would he devote that sacred head
For sinners such as I?
Was it for sins that I have done
He suffered on the tree?
Amazing pity! Grace unknown!
And love beyond degree!
But drops of grief can ne'er repay
The debt of love I owe;
Here, Lord, I give my self away—
'Tis all that I can do. Amen.

Allow teenagers 10 to 15 minutes to read and write, then ask them to fold up their paper into a square.

MAKE IT REAL

With worship music playing in the background, invite volunteers to help you lower the wooden cross at the front of the room so that it is lying flat on the ground. Invite everyone to gather around the cross, then ask teenagers to take a nail and carefully use a hammer to nail their folded paper to the cross. You could have two or three teenagers nail their commitment papers to the cross at a time.

LEADER'S LOW-DOWN:

If you have a very large group, you'll need more than one wooden cross. Set out a wooden cross at each corner of your meeting area and assign adult volunteers to supervise the hammering at each station.

When all the commitment papers are nailed to the cross, hoist it back up. Have everyone stand together, gathered in front of the cross.

SAY: Jesus knows your heart. He knows your commitment to Him. And through nailing our written responses to the cross, we're visually representing our inner commitment to take up our own crosses and die to ourselves.

Close your eyes and let me pray for you.

PRAY: Jesus, thank You for Your amazing love. Thank You for all You endured for me and for each person in this room when You died on the cross. God, I commission these warriors for You to live in total dedication and commitment. They desire to live for You, Jesus. They desire to die to the world, to die to self, to die to the power of sin. I pray that You'd help them to live in complete devotion and radical love for You. Thank You for the cross. In Jesus' name, amen.

LEADER'S LOW-DOWN:

To add extra "umph!" to this session, give students a special cross keepsake that will remind them of their commitment. To make each keepsake, use a hot glue gun to affix two nails together in the shape of the cross and tie a loop of twine at the top so students can hang the cross somewhere in their room at home. Give these crosses to teenagers as they leave the session.

LEADER'S LOW-DOWN:

At the end of this session, make sure teens return any objects they collected for the Symbol Scavenger Hunt during the warm-up activity. You will also want to recruit several adults to help you remove the nails and papers affixed to the cross. Be sure to dispose of the papers without reading them in order to protect the privacy of students.

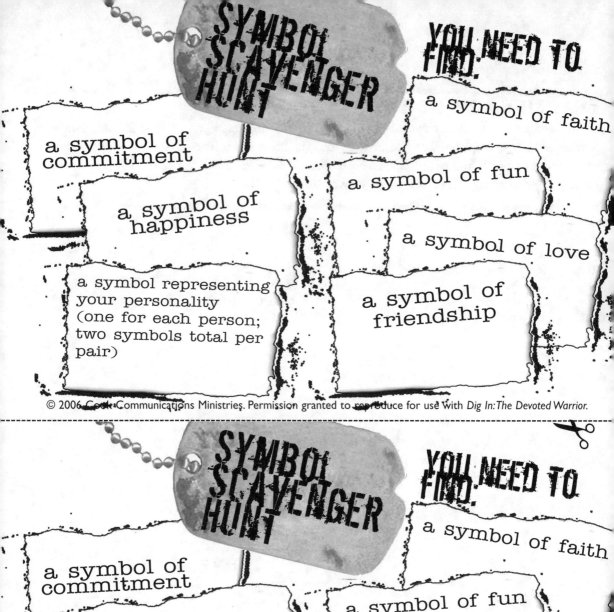

SYMBOL SCAVENGER HUNT

YOU NEED TO FIND:

a symbol of faith

a symbol of commitment

a symbol of fun

a symbol of happiness

a symbol of love

a symbol representing your personality (one for each person; two symbols total per pair)

a symbol of friendship

SYMBOL SCAVENGER HUNT

YOU NEED TO FIND:

a symbol of faith

a symbol of commitment

a symbol of fun

a symbol of happiness

a symbol of love

a symbol representing your personality (one for each person; two symbols total per pair)

a symbol of friendship

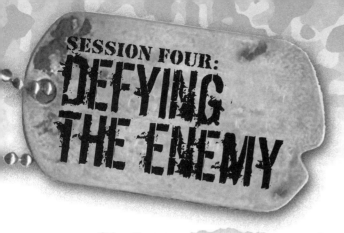

SESSION FOUR: DEFYING THE ENEMY

WHAT'S THE POINT?

As followers of Christ, we should live in a way that renounces the enemy and his values.

A QUICK GLANCE...

MINUTES	SECTION	SUPPLIES
up to 30	Optional Warm-Up Activity	Masking tape
15 to 20	A Love/Hate Relationship	Red paper hearts, black paper hearts, Bibles, sheet of newsprint, marker
25 to 35	The World vs. the Cross	Bibles, Training Manuals, pens, newsprint sheet, masking tape, marker, (Optional: pop culture and sports magazines), Dig In DVD, TV, DVD player
15 to 20	We Have an Enemy	Bibles
up to 10	My Life, My King, His Values	Training Manuals, pens, Bibles, CD player, CD of worship music or instrumentalist
10 to 15	Ministry Time	Training Manuals, Dig In DVD, TV, DVD player
up to 10	Make It Real	Large newsprint banner, a cross up front, black paper hearts, several rolls of masking tape

Before the event begins, make sure every student has his or her Training Manual. Set up the large, free-standing wooden cross near the front of your meeting area and hang a large newsprint banner that reads "The Enemy, His Values, His World" on the back wall of your meeting room (opposite the cross). Cut out black and red construction paper hearts; you'll need one of each color for every student. Set up a CD player and a CD of worship music or arrange to have a musician. Set up a TV and DVD player and be ready to play the *Dig In* DVD. If you're able, collect and bring old magazines, such as celebrity magazines, music or entertainment magazines, sports magazines, or even news magazines.

OPTIONAL WARM-UP ACTIVITY

Welcome teenagers as they arrive and divide the group into two teams for an active game. Give one team a roll of masking tape and ask them to pass it around so that each team member can put a large masking tape "X" on the front of his or her shirt.

SAY: We're going to play "Team Blob Tag." I am going to select one person to be "IT" from each team. Whoever is IT has one goal: tagging all the members of the enemy team. So, if you're on the team without Xs, you need to watch out for the IT from that team because he or she is after *you*. And vice versa—if you're on the X team, watch out for the IT from the team without Xs because he or she is after you. Got it so far?

OK, here's the catch: Once you get tagged by IT, you now become part of IT. You'll hold hands with IT and together run around the room tagging people who were on your team. You now have switched sides! Your original team is now your enemy and you're out to get them.

So, each time an IT tags someone, that person gets added onto IT. Eventually, IT will be a big chain of people holding hands, sweeping around the room trying to catch members of the enemy. Make sense?

Allow time for teenagers to ask questions, then select an IT from each team and have kids go at it. If time allows, play several rounds of the game and have students form new teams each time; this variation of team members will create confusion and make the game more fun and challenging!

If your group has 10 students or fewer, customize this game by having students play without two teams. Simply have one person be IT with the job of tagging everyone else. Each time someone is tagged, that person should join IT by holding hands and running together to tag others.

After the game, have everyone grab a Training Manual and take a seat. (Have students create rows with their chairs, facing the front of the room.)

A LOVE/HATE RELATIONSHIP

Pass out paper hearts so that each teenager gets a black one and a red one.

SAY: I'm going to name a few things and after each one I want you to hold up one of your hearts. The red heart means "Love it!" and the black heart means "Hate it!" Each time I name something, you must immediately hold up one of the hearts to show how you feel about it. As you've probably noticed, there isn't a "neutral"—you've got to vote "Love it!" or "Hate it!" for each item. Got it?

Name several items that kids can respond to, and customize your list of words using these guidelines.
- Name a gross food
- Name a popular band
- Name a local high school
- Name a local restaurant
- Name a rival professional football team
- Name a "boring" activity
- Name a recent romantic-comedy movie
- Name one of your favorite foods
- Name a favorite local sports team
- Name a nearby mall or shopping area
- Name a TV sitcom
- Name another local high school
- Name a well-known celebrity

Encourage teenagers to look around after each item to see how many red or black hearts are being held up by their peers.

After you've mentioned all the items, summarize for the group which items appeared to be the most loved and the most hated. Then **ASK:**

Was it hard to do this without a neutral vote?
Which items would you have voted "neutral" for if you could?

Collect all the hearts and set them aside for use later, then **SAY:**

When it comes to the way we feel about the world, the Bible makes it clear that there is no "neutral" ground. We're called to either love it or hate it.

Invite students to read these passages aloud while everyone else reads along: Matthew 6:24, Luke 14:26, John 12:25

Hang up a large sheet of newsprint and draw a line down the middle dividing it into two columns. Write "LOVE" over one column and "HATE" over the other. Ask teenagers to shout out what each verse said we are to love or to hate as followers of Christ, and write down what they say in the appropriate columns.

ASK: What stands out to you from these verses?
What's your reaction to these commands?

LEADER'S LOW-DOWN

Students may be confused by these verses at the outset—especially Jesus' command to hate our families! If kids have questions, encourage them to hold tight and let them know that you will be exploring these verses further during this session and helping students understand what they really mean.

SAY: In the Gospels we are bombarded with words from Jesus that address the kind of commitment a person should have when choosing to follow him. But the really interesting part is not that we are called to follow, obey, and serve Him—it is that we are called to do these things in the most dramatic fashion! For example, we are not commanded to abstain from sin—we're told to gouge out an eye and cut off a hand if it causes us to sin! Now, it should be obvious to us that Jesus is not asking us to *literally* do this. If we did, all Christians would look like pirates! Jesus' point isn't that we should actually mutilate ourselves. Instead, this is an example of hyperbole: using exaggeration to strongly emphasize an idea. Jesus' point is that we are supposed to respond violently to our sin! His real focus is on the attitude of the action, not simply the action.

Here's another example: We're not called to just "follow Jesus." Rather, He says to pick up our cross. Death! That is discipleship.

Now, here, in Matthew 6:24, Luke 14:26, and John 12:25 we are not told simply to prefer God to money, family, or self. We are told to *hate* money, family, and self. Now what's the point? When compared to our radical and all-consuming love for God, our relationship to money, family, and even to ourselves *looks* like hate. This is a brilliant rhetorical device that expresses the *kind* of commitment Jesus demands.

Christianity is not safe. It's not for the weak of heart. If someone has told you that Christianity is a crutch, a place for weak souls, then you have been lied to, plain and simple. Look at Scripture. Jesus could have had many more followers if He would have presented Christianity as such. But instead, Jesus seems to push people away with His difficult words and demands.

THE WORLD VS. THE CROSS

SAY: Let's look at a passage that emphasizes the high calling God has for His followers.

Invite a volunteer to read aloud 1 John 2:15 while everyone else reads along.

ASK: What do you think this verse means? How would you say it in your own words?

SAY: We're called not to love the world or anything in the world. In fact, this passage says, if we love the world then we aren't filled with the love of the Father. Let's check out another passage that's even more dramatic.

Invite a volunteer to read aloud James 4:4 while everyone else reads along.

SAY: We have an extreme calling—to hate the world and to love God. But what does it really mean to hate the world?

The reality is that the values of Christ—and the values of His followers—are radically different from the values and mind-set of the world. We have a stark choice to make: will we live by the values of the world? Or will we live by the values of Christ?

Let's watch a clip called "Split Passions" about a man who had just that: split passions.

Play DVD clip "Split Passions" (Length 3:38)

Okay. So he went a little overboard. But really, how often do we do the same thing: try to mix our passion for God with our desires for things of the world?

SHORT SYNOPSIS: "Split Passions"
This clip shows a youth pastor who claims to love Jesus but is TOTALLY obsessed with a boy band. Funny clip . . . relevant point.

LEADER'S LOW-DOWN

If you've brought magazines, give some to each group and invite them to flip through the magazines to look for examples of worldly values and ideas. Prompt them to use the specific examples they've found to help them answer the questions on pages 14–15 in their Training Manual.

Get together in groups of four and turn to pages 14–15 in your Training Manual. I want you to take 15 minutes to work together to discuss the questions and take notes, exploring together how the values of the world differ from the values of Jesus.

After 10 minutes, invite groups to summarize what they discussed about the meaning of 1 John 2:15. Then hang up another large newsprint sheet and draw a line down the center creating two columns. Write "The World's Values" above one column and "God's Values" above the other column. Ask the group to share the ideas they came up with for each of the following categories and write them on the chart:

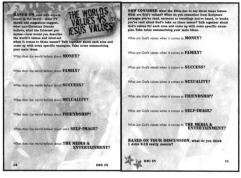

- **Money**
- **Family**
- **Success**
- **Sexuality**
- **Friendship**
- **Self-Image**
- **Media/Entertainment**

Once the chart is filled, **SAY:**

Great job! It is really clear from our chart that God's values are totally different than the world's. Sometimes the real-life choices we are faced with are totally obvious. For example, if someone is pushing us to try drugs, it is pretty clear that God doesn't want us to do that. If we're tempted with sex outside of marriage, we need to remember that Scripture is clear: absolutely not. If we're tempted to use violence against someone we're angry at, the Bible is black and white on this topic: no way!

But it isn't always that easy to know how to live out God's values instead of the world's. For example, how do you demonstrate God's values when it comes to movies, music, or TV shows? Does 1 John 2:15 mean that we can't like or enjoy *anything* that's secular? Or what about God's values for sexuality—does living out God's values mean that we never kiss, hold hands, or even date? When it comes to money, does living by God's values mean we literally give away all our money to the poor and never buy anything for ourselves?

If we don't want to be influenced by the world, does that mean that we should hole ourselves up in Christian communities and never talk to non-Christians? Does it mean that we live by a system of legalistic rules? When it comes down to the practical issues of life, how do we know what it *really means* to hate the world's values and love God's instead?

Let's get into the Bible for some guidance. Several Scripture passages can help us understand the standards we should set for ourselves when it comes to how we relate to the things of this world.

Ask a volunteer to read aloud Philippians 4:4–8 while everyone else follows along in their own Bibles.

SAY: When we're faced with a gray area, like watching a certain movie, listening to a certain band, or hanging out with certain friends, we can use Philippians 4:4–8 to ask ourselves some important questions: Will participating in this activity lead me to rejoice in the Lord? Will it cause me to be a more gentle person? Will it lead me toward worry and stress or toward God's peace? Will it fill my mind with thoughts that are true, noble, pure, lovely, admirable, and excellent? If you ask yourself these questions—and you're really honest with yourself—those "grays" turn out to be a little more black and white than you thought. If you know that an activity won't help you live out the principles in Philippians 4:4–8, then chances are you probably shouldn't do it.

Let's look at another passage.

Prompt a volunteer to read aloud Galatians 5:19–24 while everyone else reads along.

SAY: The first part of this passage clearly points out some of the values and behaviors of the world. The second part—the fruit of the Spirit—highlights God's values. When you're facing a choice, you can simply ask yourself if that action will help you grow in love, in joy, in peace, in patience, in kindness, in goodness, in faithfulness, in gentleness, and in self-control. If the answer is "no," well then you probably shouldn't do it.

Let's check out one more Scripture.

Invite a volunteer to read aloud John 16:7–11 while everyone else follows along.

SAY: This is the most important source of truth for us when we're trying to live out God's values: the Holy Spirit! If you are a Christian, the Holy Spirit is within you. And as Jesus explained in this passage, the Holy Spirit works in us to convict us of sin and to point us to righteousness. If we sincerely desire to do what's right, we simply need to listen to the Holy Spirit. God will point us in the right direction . . . *and* He'll convict us if we're making the wrong choice. We simply need to have a heart that desires to listen and obey.

Return to the chart and **SAY:**

So when we live in a world whose values are totally contrary to God, there's just no way around it: Following Jesus demands that we renounce the world. We declare that we're citizens of a different kingdom. We follow our King—and we refuse to take part in the distorted values of this world.

WE HAVE AN ENEMY

SAY: Imagine this scenario—you're watching the news and you hear this report: The government has just declared that based on surveillance and undercover intelligence, they've discovered that the small town in which you live is a home base for a dangerous terrorist group. In fact, the mayor of your town, the school board, and the teachers in the schools are all members of the group. The newspaper, the books, the radio stations—everything is controlled by this group. Furthermore, it appears that the terrorist group is planning to blow up all the non-terrorist parts of your town! You're shocked, you're scared, you don't know what to do. But then you hear something even more shocking.

They show a news reporter on a street corner interviewing a teenager from your school. He says, "Well, *I'm* not a terrorist. But, hey, I do like the music they play. I mean, what's wrong with that? They also dress really cool—so what's the big deal if I like their style? And I do like their teachings. I mean, I don't actually *agree* with their ideas, but some of their suggestions aren't so bad. What's the big deal? Just because I like some of their ideas doesn't mean I'm one of them!"

That's totally ludicrous! No one in their right mind would admire and mimic behaviors and ideas of terrorists and act like it isn't a big deal! And though the scenario I described would never really happen, a situation a lot like it happens all the time.

Throughout Christian history, followers of Christ used to declare: "I renounce the devil and all his empty promises . . . ." But now some Christians don't even believe the devil exists. And others believe he exists, but they're not able to recognize his influence in this world. We don't just have a vague or general enemy—we have a specific one: Satan. We have to admit that there's someone we're fighting against before we can begin to fight!

The reality is that just like the illustration I shared, we do have an enemy—and we live in his territory, whether we realize it or not. And we have a choice to make: do we mimic the enemy's values, live with the enemy's mind-set, and then think it's no big deal? Or do we choose to recognize our enemy, defy his strategy, and live totally for God?

Let's look at one of the names Jesus had for Satan, our enemy.

Invite volunteers to read aloud John 12:31–32, 14:30, and 16:8–11.

SAY: Jesus called Satan the "prince of this world" because he is the source of the worldly values and mind-set we've been talking about. God has allowed Satan to have power in this world. In fact, Jesus Himself described a battle for souls between Satan and God. Look what Jesus said to Paul when he was on the road to Damascus.

Read aloud Acts 26:15–18.

SAY: When Paul put his faith in Jesus, he went from being under Satan's power to being under the power of God.

When we ignore this battle—when we forget whose side we're on and we instead buy into worldly values—we're giving our enemy a foothold in our lives. Think back to the game we played at the beginning of our session. If you would've just sat there, ignoring what was really going on, you would've gotten tagged in no time! Similarly, people who live lives unaware of the reality of an enemy—ignorant of the battle between Satan's values and God's—are bound to fall prey to the enemy's attacks.

But hey! We're not powerless! By choosing to live by God's values and to defy the prince of this world and his schemes, we can have power to fight the enemy!

Invite volunteers to read aloud Ephesians 4:25–28, 6:10–13; James 4:7–10; and 1 Peter 5:8–9.

SAY: You are a warrior for Christ! You can defy the enemy by hanging onto God's truth, by living out God's values, by fighting for His kingdom!

MY LIFE, MY KING, HIS VALUES

SAY: So what about you? What about *your* life? Are you living with worldly values? Have you bought into a worldly mind-set? How has Satan been getting a foothold in your life? I'd like us each to take some time alone to evaluate our own lives. So find a private space in the room, then turn to page 16 in your Training Manual and use the questions there to guide your own personal evaluation. You've got about 10 minutes.

LEADER'S LOW-DOWN:

FYI—on page 16 in their Training Manuals, students will respond to a series of questions that prompt them to identify areas in their own life in which they've allowed the world to influence them. Teenagers will be challenged to give up their love for the world and worldly things and focus entirely on their love for Christ.

Play a CD of worship music (or have a musician play music) while teenagers are writing. After ten minutes, invite everyone to gather back together.

MINISTRY TIME

Ask everyone to reform their groups of four from "The World vs. The Cross" activity. **SAY: Now that you've spent time individually committing to change, we're going to spend some time in community sharing with each other how God has been speaking to us and encouraging each other in our faith commitments. Turn to page 17 in your Training Manual and talk through the questions together. Then pray together, asking God to help you renounce the world.**

LEADER'S LOW-DOWN:

During their small group discussion, groups will read and talk about the paraphrase of I John 2:15–17 in Eugene Peterson's *The Message*. Here is a copy of the text for your convenience: "Don't love the world's ways. Don't love the world's goods. Love of the world squeezes out love for the Father. Practically everything that goes on in the world—wanting your own way, wanting everything for yourself, wanting to appear important—has nothing to do with the Father. It just isolates you from him. The world and all its wanting, wanting, wanting is on the way out—but whoever does what God wants is set for eternity."

Allow groups 10 to 15 minutes to discuss the questions and pray together, then invite everyone to gather back together as a large group.

SAY: Renouncing the world and clinging to the cross is far from easy. But we have within us the power of God! Can you imagine an entire generation united together—talk about God's power! It's gonna be an all-out revolution!

Play DVD clip "Revolution" (Length 3:36)

SHORT SYNOPSIS: "Revolution"

This inspiring clip shows the dire state of today's world then challenges teens to take action and take back their generation for Christ.

MAKE IT REAL

Pass out the black hearts again so that everyone has one, and put several rolls of masking tape on the floor near the banner at the back of the room reading, "The Enemy, His Values, His World."

SAY: Let's all stand, turn, and face the back of the room. (Wait for everyone to do so, then continue.) **We face a choice: do we live by the enemy's values?**

Read aloud all the ideas listed on under "The World's Values" from the chart students created in "The World vs. The Cross."

SAY: We reject those ideas and that mind-set. We choose to hate the things of this world.

Invite students to repeat aloud together:

I renounce the devil and all his empty promises.

Then prompt them to tape their black hearts—symbolizing hatred—onto the banner. When they're done, have them gather in the middle again and ask them to turn their backs to the banner so that they are now facing the cross.

Invite them to repeat aloud together:

I turn my back on the enemy's values and his lies.
I choose the way of Christ.

Ask students to remain standing facing the cross as you pray:

Father God, You are our King. We live solely for You. Help us to renounce the world. Help us to identify the schemes of the enemy and defy his efforts to turn us from You. Empower us to listen to Your Holy Spirit and to make right choices based on Your leading. Give us the courage to give up habits or activities that we know are not pleasing to You. We want to live by Your values. We pray these things in Jesus' name, amen.

LEADER'S LOW-DOWN:
Keep the newsprint banner from "The World vs. the Cross" activity; you'll use it in Session Five.

SESSION FIVE:
HIS AGENTS

WHAT'S THE POINT?

As God's agents, we live out His mission in the world by loving others and sharing the Gospel.

A QUICK GLANCE . . .

MINUTES	SECTION	SUPPLIES
up to 30	Optional Warm-Up Activity	Toothpicks, gumdrops, paper cups, masking tape, aluminum foil, mini-marshmallows, cloth sheet, paper bags
15 to 20	Not Quite Undercover	Slips of paper (prepared in advance—see below), "The World's Values/God's Values" newsprint sheet from Session Four, Training Manuals
30 to 35	More to "The World" Than Meets the Eye	Training Manuals, Bibles
15 to 20	Our True Citizenship	Training Manuals, Bibles
15 to 20	Your Mission, Should You Choose to Accept It	Training Manuals, pens, Dig In DVD, TV, DVD player
10 to 15	Ministry Time	Photocopies of maps, rolls of masking tape, a large wooden cross up front
5 to 10	Make It Real	Training Manuals

Before the session begins, create a model using toothpicks, gumdrops, paper cups, masking tape, and strips of aluminum foil; it should be an intricate creation, like a building, or an abstract version of a dog, or even an awkward attempt at a double helix—anything you want! See the example on the next page.

Keep the model top secret by covering it with a sheet and setting it aside. In a paper bag, put all the supplies each team of students will need to create their own mimicked version of your model. You'll need one paper bag with all necessary supplies for every three teenagers.

Be sure also to set up a TV and DVD player and be ready to play the *Dig In* DVD.

Also, photocopy and cut apart slips of paper. You can make your own or photocopy page 90 at the end of this session. (Photocopying privileges are given for page 90 only.) You may also choose to download the Game Slips from http://downloads.battlecry.com.

Half of the slips should read:
You're UNDERCOVER: Each time you shake someone's hand, give it a subtle extra squeeze.

The rest of the slips should read:
Just be yourself and follow the leader's instructions.

In addition, make sure you've got the newsprint sheet from Session Four that listed "The World's Values" and "God's Values" in two columns.

For the concluding activities, you'll need a large wooden cross set up in the front of the room. You'll also need to create 8 1/2 x 11 inch sheets of paper which have a map copied onto one side. You can photocopy a world map, a country map, or even state or regional maps for this. You'll need enough map photocopies so that each student can have one.

Make sure every student has his or her Training Manual.

OPTIONAL WARM-UP ACTIVITY

Welcome teenagers as they arrive and have them divide into teams of three. Bring out your model—still covered with a sheet—and set it in the front.

SAY: Under this cloth I have a very unique work of art, created by yours truly! Your job is to work together as sculptors in your trio to create an exact replica of my model. I'll give you all the supplies you'll need. Sound easy? Keep listening. . .

Here's the challenge: Your trio must find a location outside of this room in which you'll create your replica.

LEADER'S LOW-DOWN:

Depending on your location, you may want to give specific instructions for where students should go. For example, you could send them to certain Sunday school rooms or tell them that they must be at least 25 yards from your room. Try to specify a location that will cause students to get a little exercise as they run back and forth to look at the sculpture.

Once you've found a spot to work, you can send one runner back to this room who can take a look at my sculpture. The runner can look at it as long as he or she wants, and then can run back and describe to the rest of the team what it looks like. The other two sculptors then need to start working together to create a replica using the supplies I've given you.

The trio can keep sending runners back to look at the sculpture, and each person can take turns being the runner—the only stipulation is that only one runner from a team can be in this room at a time. Make sense?

Your trio's goal is to work together to make a sculpture that is an *exact* replica of mine, down to the tiniest detail.

LEADER'S LOW-DOWN:

Make sure the sculpture you've created is intricate enough that it will take students at least 15 minutes to copy it. Include small details such as wrapping some of the toothpicks in foil, alternating between gumdrops and marshmallows, etc.

When everyone understands the idea of the game, send trios out to pick their spots, then uncover your sculpture so runners can observe it.

When a trio feels they've gotten an exact replica, encourage them to send a runner one more time to double-check all the details. If they're confident, invite them to carefully carry their model back into the meeting room and wait until all the groups have finished.

(If one or two trios are taking a lot longer than everyone else, give them a time limit such as "You've got three more minutes!")

When all the groups are done, invite them to compare and contrast all the various sculptures and the model. Congratulate groups on their accuracy, attention to detail, and teamwork.

If you have extra time, invite trios to deconstruct their models and then create their own sculptures. Encourage them to be creative and make anything they want!

Afterward, have teenagers toss out their sculptures and gather in the middle of the room.

NOT QUITE UNDERCOVER

SAY: We're going to play another quick game. I'm going to give you a slip of paper and I want you to quietly read it and then keep its contents an absolute secret.

Shuffle and pass out the slips of paper you prepared. Once everyone has read their slip, **SAY: Now take five minutes to mingle with everybody in the room. Greet each person with a handshake, say hi, and then tell them quickly about the best thing that happened to you during the week.**

Here's the catch: some of you are undercover agents. If you are an agent, your job is to try to reveal your identity to other

under-cover agents by following the instructions on your slip. But you also need to avoid being detected by non-agents! So you need to be sneaky and subtle. If you think you've identified another agent, just keep it to yourself—we'll reveal our guesses at the end of the game.

And for those of you who *aren't* undercover agents, your job is to try to identify who might be an undercover agent. Look for clues in how people act and what they do when you speak with them. Again, if you think you've identified another agent, don't say any-thing—wait 'til the end of the game.

When everyone understands the basic idea, prompt kids to mingle with each other for five minutes. When time's up, have teenagers each grab a chair and take a seat. (Have students create rows with their chairs, facing the front of the room.)

Invite everyone to call out their guesses about who was or was not a secret agent. After most teenagers have guessed, invite all the under-cover agents to stand up and identify themselves.

ASK the group: **Was it easy or hard to tell who was an under-cover agent?**
Who was easiest to guess?
Which of you were hardest to guess?

SAY: Let me tell you a story about somebody who was the ulti-mate undercover agent.[7]

Joe Pistone was an FBI agent in the 1970s when he got what seemed like an impossible assignment: infiltrating the mafia. Pistone, who grew up around the mob, was up for the challenge. He created an alias for himself—Donnie Brasco—and made up a past as a jewel thief. And after some work, he got in. He talked the talk, he walked the walk—he was accepted as a member of the Bonnano crime family.

Joe Pistone was so good at what he did that he was part of the mafia for six years. Did you hear that? *Six years!* He lived, moved, and breathed among some of the scariest tough guys in the country, and yet they didn't suspect him. We can only imagine some of the dark deeds Pistone had to do in order to be accepted by the mob—for them to believe he was one of them. He once was even asked to "whack" somebody—to *kill* an enemy of the mob. Luckily, Pistone was able to avoid blowing his cover because the person disappeared!

Eventually things started to get really heated in the Bonnano family. When conflict in the family led to three murders, the FBI decided it was too dangerous for Pistone to continue.

So after six years in the mafia, Pistone broke his cover—and he took down hundreds of mafia members! His testimony put over 120 mafia members in prison for life.

Okay, now think about this for a minute. Imagine how deep you'd have to go into the mafia—into leading a double-life—for them to accept you as one of them…for *six years!* What did Pistone have to compromise in order to keep up his fake criminal identity? And though he did take down 120 mafiosi with him, we've got to wonder: at what price? What was the mental and emotional toll of living like a mob member for six years? Was the line ever blurred between pretending to be a criminal and actually thinking like one—actually *becoming* one?

LEADER'S LOW-DOWN:

Some teenagers might recognize this story; there's a film about Joe Pistone's life called *Donnie Brasco* and starring Johnny Depp. The film *Donnie Brasco* contains violent images and nudity, so if students bring it up, be prepared to advise students against watching it based on the principles they learned in Session Four.

Like Joe Pistone, each of us has been given a mission. Each of us is God's agent in this world. We're not called to infiltrate a crime family—we're called to infiltrate the world for God. Yet sadly, many of us live out the mission just like Joe did. We keep our true identity a secret. We mimic the ways of the world around us. We blend right in. We take our faith undercover.

But the truth is, our mission is *not* like Joe's. We're not called to blend in. We're not to live secret, hidden Christian lives. There should be no mistaking who we really are. We should stand out by the way we live. People should immediately see a difference in us.

Hold up "The World's Values/God's Values" newsprint sheet from Session Four and read aloud some of "The World's Values."

SAY: Does the way we live and the words we say lead people to think we live by this system? Or is our identity as God's agents obvious, as we embrace His values?

Read aloud some of "God's Values" from the chart, then **SAY:**
If we live these out, we definitely *won't* blend in with the world around us. Do you remember what Scripture said about the world?

Ask volunteers to read aloud 1 John 2:15–16 and 1 John 4:4.

Then ask students to turn to page 18 in their Training Manuals on which they'll find the following diagram:

Love the World   Love God
<————————————————————————————————>
(hate God)   (hate the world)

SAY: When we're friends with the world—with Satan's values and his agenda—then we're making ourselves enemies of God. But as we move toward love for God, we also begin to understand what it means to hate the world—to reject the values of our enemy. As you can see on the diagram in your Training Manual, we can't have it both ways. If we start to love the values of this world, then we're moving away from true love of God. We need to choose instead to reject the values and temptations of the world and focus fully on our commitment to God.

MORE TO THE WORLD THAN MEETS THE EYE

SAY: But as we're talking about the world and its values, it's important to remember that the phrase "the world" actually has several different meanings in Scripture. One of those meanings is the one we just discussed: Satan's power and his agenda. Let's read a few more Scriptures that focus on this meaning of the phrase "the world."

Invite volunteers to read aloud the following passages:
John 15:18–19
John 16:33
James 1:27
1 John 3:13

ASK: What stood out to you from those passages?

Affirm students' observations, then **SAY:**
In Scripture there are also some positive meanings for the phrase "the world." First, in Scripture "the world" can mean this planet and the awesome universe God created! Let's read some passages that talk about the world in this way.

Ask volunteers to read aloud the following passages:
Genesis 1:31–2:1
Matthew 25:34
John 1:9–10
Acts 17:24

SAY: The fact of the matter is that we live on this planet—we live in this world. God put us here on this earth, and He has a purpose for us here. So when we talk about hating the world, we're not talking about hating God's creation. We should love God's creation and praise God for the amazing world He made! When we talk about hating the world, we're talking specifically about hating Satan's values and a worldly mind-set.

There's another meaning of the phrase "the world" in Scripture, and it refers to the *people* of this world. The Bible is clear: God *loves* the world. God doesn't love the *values* of the world, but he passionately loves the *people* of the world.

I'd like you to get into groups of three or four. In your small groups, turn to pages 19–20 in your Training Manual and take some time to read the directions and discuss the Scripture passages.

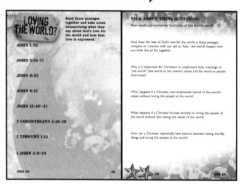

Allow groups 15 to 20 minutes to read Scripture and discuss the questions on pages 19–20 of their Training Manuals, then have everyone gather back together and **ASK** the group:
Which passage stood out to you the most? Why?
How would you summarize God's loving plan for the world based on what you read?
How can a Christian balance hatred for worldly values and love for the people of the world? What would that look like?

SAY: It is so important that as Christians we understand how we are to relate to the world. We are to reject the values of Satan and his power; we are to care for the physical world God created; and we are to share God's heart of love for the people of the world.

OUR TRUE CITIZENSHIP

SAY: Have you ever had one of those moments when you didn't feel quite at home in this world? You looked around you—at the values of our culture, at the loneliness and emptiness people feel—and you just knew in your heart that you didn't belong?

LEADER'S LOW-DOWN

At this point, you might want to share a recent example from your own life of a time when you felt the tension between living in this world but being a citizen of a different world.

Invite volunteers to read aloud Ephesians 2:19 and Philippians 3:20.

SAY: The reality is that as Christians we are God's agents in this world. Though we live on this planet, our true citizenship is somewhere else. We belong to God and His Kingdom.

Ask volunteers to read aloud Hebrews 11:13 and 1 Peter 2:11.

SAY: We're aliens, but not in the E.T., outer-space sense. We're aliens and strangers in the sense that we're from another place, we belong to another kingdom, our allegiance is to our Lord, and we live according to His values. We're not *meant* to feel at home in this world.

The British writer G.K. Chesterton understood well the strange relationship between a Christian and the world. He wrote, "One must somehow find a way of loving the world without trusting it; somehow one must love the world without being worldly."[8] It's a strange paradox, but it's right on—we must love the world without becoming worldly ourselves.

There's another great quote I love that also addresses the Christian's paradoxical relationship to the world. In their song "This World," Caedmon's Call says, "This world has nothing for me and this world has everything—all that I could want and nothing that I need."[9]

What does this mean for *you*? If you're a citizen of heaven, how are you to live in this world? How do you relate to the people of this world, the values of this world, the good and bad enticements of this world?

DIG IN LEADER'S GUIDE

Turn to a partner and talk through the questions on page 21 in your Training Manual. We'll get back together in five minutes.

After five minutes, invite volunteers to share their thoughts from their pair discussion and affirm their observations.

SAY: Webster's Dictionary defines the word *patriot* as "one who loves and loyally supports one's country." And it seems that this may be the most accurate word to describe the situation of Christians. We are patriots of God's kingdom. And according to Scripture, being patriots of God's kingdom *makes us* patriots of this world. We find that our love for the other world—for God's heavenly kingdom—has made us committed to this one. We reflect and model God's love for the *people* of this world without loving and embracing the *values* of this world.

YOUR MISSION SHOULD YOU CHOOSE TO ACCEPT IT

SAY: As Christians, we find ourselves in a strange position. First, we're told in Scripture to renounce this world and all it offers. Second, we're told that this world is not our true home. We belong to a different kind of place, a different sort of government, and a different code of ethics. We're citizens of a holy, invisible kingdom. And though these two ideas are essential to our understanding of reality as Christians, there is a third idea that we need to contend with: we *are* residents in this world. It is a world that God loves, a world that God desires to save, and most importantly, a world in which we have a responsibility. As God's agents on this planet, we need to live out the mission that God has for us!

God's mission for us has two parts: the first focuses on how we should *live* and the second on what we are to *do*.

Scripture is clear that part of our mission during our lives on this planet is to live in a way that points others to God. We are to live pure and holy lives so that others can see the pure and holy God through us.

Invite volunteers to read aloud the following passages:

Matthew 5:14
2 Corinthians 1:12
1 Peter 2:11

Then **SAY:** **To shine as lights for Christ, we need to live in such a way towards non-Christians that they say, "Hey, something is different about you!" We should be so kind, so loving, so honest and true, that they discover in us genuine friendship and the sincere love of God. Our lives should be like magnets, attracting others to God. Just like the game we played at the beginning of this session, we are to live as replicas of God and His values. We are to model our behavior and our choices after God's Word. When people look at us, they should see an image of God and what He's like.**

Now I know that none of us is perfect—we *will* mess up. And when we do, we need to acknowledge it, ask forgiveness, and move forward.

Remember that old Sunday school song, "This Little Light of Mine"? One of the verses says, "Hide it under a bushel? No! I'm gonna let it shine!" A bushel is like a bowl or a basket that one can put over a candle to hide its light. In essence, that verse is talking about undercover faith. Are you going to live in a way that hides your faith, that covers your light, so that you blend in with the darkness of the world? Or are you going to live brilliantly, shining brightly, through your conduct and everyday choices pointing the way to the true light of the world: Jesus?

This is your mission—to live as lights.

And the second part of your mission is to carry out some specific instructions from God. Let's see what it is that God wants us to *do*.

Invite volunteers to read aloud the following Scriptures:

Matthew 28:19–20
Mark 16:15
2 Corinthians 5:18–20.

SAY: We are part of God's plan for this world—we are His agents, declaring His message to the non-Christians around us. We are to preach the Gospel in all the world, whether it's in our neighborhood, our school, or across the globe. God's plan—to reconcile lost sinners to Himself—is underway, and we are His ambassadors in this world, showing and telling others how to experience reconciliation with God and become citizens of His kingdom.

Play DVD clip "Audio Adrenaline: 'Hands and Feet'" (Length 3:35)

> **SHORT SYNOPSIS:**
> **"Audio Adrenaline: 'Hands and Feet'"**
>
> This music video features the Christian group Audio Adrenaline and their song "Hands and Feet." It shows followers of Christ living out the call to missions.

Some people like to live out a quote that is sometimes attributed to St. Francis of Assisi. You may have heard it before—it goes, "Preach the Gospel at all times. If necessary, use words." There *is* an important truth in this idea, and we just talked about it: the truth that our actions and the way we live are a critical part of our faith. But there's one major flaw in this quote—it implies that using words to share our faith is only sometimes necessary. That simply *isn't true*. Scripture is clear that we are to preach the Gospel, that we are to be God's witnesses, that we need to tell our friends the good news about Jesus. We can live good, righteous lives for 80 years, but if we never actually *tell* anyone about Jesus, then we've failed! Our mission involves both actions and words. As we rely on the Holy Spirit to prompt us, and as we develop relationships with non-Christians, we will know the right time to tell them about Jesus. We should never let fear or excuses keep us back from living out this part of our mission: we have *good news* to share! God loves your friends and your family! Through understanding their sin, through faith in Jesus' death on the cross and His resurrection, through a commitment to live for Him, your friends can discover a fulfilling life, their true purpose, and eternity in heaven with God.

Living like light and sharing God's message—this is your mission. Do you accept it? Will you be the hands and feet of Jesus?

MINISTRY TIME

Pass out the papers you prepared which have a map photocopied onto one side; give one to each student. Then invite students to form pairs and discuss these questions.

ASK: What is one area of your life in which you need to strive harder to be a light in this world? Be specific.

Who is someone in your life that you need to talk to about Jesus?

Based on all we've talked about, what is one action step you want to commit to take in order to live out your mission in this world?

Prompt teenagers to write down their commitment on the blank side of their paper, then ask pairs to take a few minutes to pray about the action step each person desires to take.

MAKE IT REAL

Invite teenagers to gather around the large wooden cross in the front and work together to wrap the cross with their papers, using tape to affix their papers map-side-out to the cross. Soon, the cross will look like a collage of overlapping map images.

Once the cross is covered in map images, have everyone stand in a circle around it.

LEADER'S LOW-DOWN:

If you have a really large group, you'll have way too many papers to do this effectively. Instead, have teenagers clear the chairs out of the center of the room and invite teenagers to overlap their maps on the floor to create one large cross shape, signifying all their commitments.

SAY: "For God so loved the world that he gave his one and only son, that whoever believes in him shall not perish but have eternal life. For God did not send his Son into the world to condemn the world, but to save the world through him" (John 3:16–17). This is God's plan of love for the world, that people would find forgiveness, grace, and eternal life in the cross. And you are His ambassadors, His agents on this planet, working for God to spread the good news. As you live out your mission, you are part of God's ultimate mission of love—saving the lost.

As you look at the cross, think about your part in God's mission. Think about your commitment to put that mission into action.

Let's pray.

Invite students to pray silently or aloud, worshiping God for His love and asking God to give them the courage they need to fulfill His mission for them on this planet.

LEADER'S LOW-DOWN:

After the session, recruit adult volunteers to help you remove all the maps and tape from the cross. Dispose of the papers without reading them in order to protect students' privacy.

FOR SESSION FIVE OPTIONAL WARM-UP ACTIVITY

(You may photocopy this page and cut up slips, one for each student.)

You're **UNDERCOVER:**
Each time you shake someone's hand, give it a subtle extra squeeze.

You're **UNDERCOVER:**
Each time you shake someone's hand, give it a subtle extra squeeze.

You're **UNDERCOVER:**
Each time you shake someone's hand, give it a subtle extra squeeze.

You're **UNDERCOVER:**
Each time you shake someone's hand, give it a subtle extra squeeze.

JUST BE YOURSELF and follow the leader's instructions.

JUST BE YOURSELF and follow the leader's instructions.

JUST BE YOURSELF and follow the leader's instructions.

JUST BE YOURSELF and follow the leader's instructions.

SESSION SIX:

COURAGE UNDER FIRE

WHAT'S THE POINT?

God wants us to live in courage and strength, choosing to do what's right no matter what.

A QUICK GLANCE...

MINUTES	SECTION	SUPPLIES
up to 30	Optional Warm-Up Activity	None
15 to 20	Courage Quandaries	Training Manuals, pens
15 to 20	Portraits of Courage	Training Manuals, large newsprint banner, markers, Dig In DVD, TV, DVD player
20 to 25	Wanted: Courage	Training Manuals, Bibles, pens, CD player, instrumental music CD, Dig In DVD, TV, DVD player
15 to 20	The Fear Factor	Bibles
up to 15	Ministry Time	Newsprint banner, a cross up front, Training Manuals, Bibles
up to 10	Make It Real	Candles with drip guards, basket, matches, (Optional: **Trading My Sorrows: The Best of Darrell Evans** CD)

Before the event begins, make sure every teenager has his or her Training Manual. Set up a large, free-standing wooden cross near the front of your meeting area and ready a CD player with worshipful instrumental music. Also, set up a TV and DVD player and cue up the *Dig In* DVD.

Tape a large newsprint banner (about ten feet long) on one wall in your meeting area and put several piles of colored markers on the floor in front of it. Collect small candles (one per student) and put a paper drip guard on each one. Set the candles in a basket for use at the end of the session.

OPTIONAL WARM-UP ACTIVITY

Welcome teenagers as they arrive and have everyone gather in the middle of the room.

SAY: Before we launch into our study, I want to get your opinions on some topics. I'm going to give you two choices. Each time I'll point to one of the walls in the room to represent each choice. I want you to vote for the one you think is better by going to stand against that wall. Got it?

LEADER'S LOW-DOWN:

You can play this game quickly in 10 minutes or less by following the directions as they're written. Or, if you want to expand the game and give teenagers an even greater opportunity to get to know each other, add this extra element of discussion. After each vote, have teenagers pair up with someone standing near them on their wall and take a minute or two to tell each other why they answered as they did. Encourage them to share experiences, memories, hobbies, or tastes that served as their rationale for their decision. When most pairs are done chatting, call out the next choice and have students vote again. Repeat the exercise of having them pair up and chat each time.

Use the following pairs, each time pointing to two opposite walls for students to go to in order to voice their opinion:

Pizza or steak?
Cars or motorcycles?
Dogs or cats?
Football or basketball?
Surfing or sunbathing?
Going to a play or going to a movie?
Reading books or watching TV?
Cooking food or ordering fast food?
Playing board games or playing video games?
Staying up late or waking up early?
Kindergarten or high school?
Chocolate or vanilla?
Running or swimming?
Playing a musical instrument or listening to a CD?
Summer Olympics or Winter Olympics?
Cake or pie?
Going camping or going on a cruise?
Hot dogs or hamburgers?
Science class or math class?
Emailing or talking on the phone?

After each vote, comment about the results, noting if the group was split about so-so or if a majority of students picked one of the answers.

When you're done, have everyone grab a Training Manual and a pen. Prompt kids to also find a seat. (Have students create rows with their chairs, facing the front of the room.)

COURAGE QUANDARIES

SAY: Now I'd like to get your opinions about another important topic: courage. On page 22 in your Training Manual, you'll find six questions. Each one describes two different scenarios that

require courage. Take a few minutes to quietly read each question and circle your answer for each one. You've got five minutes to pick your answers.

For your reference, here are the choices students have:

1. DOES IT TAKE MORE COURAGE...

...to skydive?   or   ...to eat worms?

2. DOES IT TAKE MORE COURAGE...

...to sing a solo in front   or   ...to climb a 50-foot ladder?
of 200 people?

3. DOES IT TAKE MORE COURAGE...

...to apologize?   or   ...to forgive?

4. DOES IT TAKE MORE COURAGE...

...to pray in public?   or   ...to publically show kindness to a social outcast?

5. DOES IT TAKE MORE COURAGE...

...for someone in a country   or   ...for a teenager in America
without freedom of religion   to stand up for Jesus even
to stand up for Jesus even   if it means losing all
if it means he'll go to prison?   her friends?

6. DOES IT TAKE MORE COURAGE...

...to go up to a stranger and   or   ...to talk openly with a good
talk to him or her about your   friend (who's not a Christian)
faith in Jesus?   about your faith in Jesus?

Allow students up to five minutes to mark all their answers.

SAY: Now let's take some time to talk about your answers. Get together in groups of three and talk about each question, explaining to each other why you answered as you did.

Give small groups up to 10 minutes to talk through the questions, then have everyone gather back together.

ASK: Did you think these were hard choices? If so, which ones were toughest?
How similar were your responses?
Were there any answers that you disagreed about? If so, what were they?

ASK: I'd like to get an idea of what our group thinks over all, so let's see a show of hands. How many of you picked praying in public as your answer for number four?
(Wait for a show of hands, and then comment about the amount of students—most of you, about half of you, or just some of you.)

ASK: What about question five—how many thought it takes more courage for an American teenager to stand up for Jesus?

(Again, comment aloud about the number of students who raise their hands.)

ASK: And for number six, how many of you thought it takes greater courage to talk to a stranger about your faith?

(Observe how many students have raised their hands.)

SAY: There are lots of opinions out there about what courage really means. Does it mean fearlessness or recklessness? Does it mean doing things that are bold and dramatic? Does it include doing things that are quiet and unnoticed? Does it mean laughing in the face of danger? What does it *really* mean for a Christian to live courageously?

PORTRAITS OF COURAGE

Play DVD clip "Abandoned" (Length 3:58)

SAY: Courage can look a lot of different ways. You just saw images of believers who paid the ultimate price for following Christ.

Let me tell you about someone who exemplifies what courage really means. Roy Pontoh[10] was an Indonesian Christian who had just attended a Christian camp. When the camp was done, Roy and some of his friends were waiting for a ride when an angry mob

SHORT SYNOPSIS: "Abandoned"

This somber but inspiring clip shows stories and images of martyrs throughout the ages. It challenges teens to abandon themselves completely for the sake of Christ.

arrived. Roy and his friends tried to hide, but eventually the mob found Roy. They told him they'd kill him if he didn't deny his faith. Roy refused, by saying, "I am a soldier of Christ!" Roy was then stabbed by one of the attackers and he died for his courage. Roy Pontoh was just 15 years old.

Allow a moment for the story to sink in.

SAY: Let me tell you about someone else who's also an awesome portrait of courage. Julie Moore[11] was a high schooler in Indiana. Julie was a Christian and sometimes other teenagers made fun of her for her faith. One day she felt sure God was calling her to start a Christian Bible study club at her school. She met with school leaders and got permission to start the club. At the first club meeting, 17 other Christians showed up. Julie was excited! But then things got tough. Gossip and mockery about the club started to spread around school. Then some students started complaining to the principal about the club, unhappy that a religious group was able to meet on campus and even get featured in the yearbook. As a result, some of the club's privileges were revoked, but they were able to keep meeting. Throughout the rest of Julie's time at her high school, the Christian club kept meeting . . . and they continued to face opposition from students who made fun of them.

Julie's story isn't as dramatic as Roy's. She never faced an angry mob. She never was threatened with death. But just like Roy, Julie lived in courage. Courage doesn't just mean bravely facing danger—it means something more.

Let's take a look at some of the ways people define courage. Get back together in your groups of three and turn to page 23 in your Training Manual. Read all the quotes about courage, then I want each of you to pick a quote that *you* think best defines what courage means. Share your choice with your group, then follow the rest of the instructions on that page.

When groups are done, gather everyone again and invite a representative from each group to read aloud their "courage means" statement and affirm their good ideas.

SAY: Here's one way I like to define courage. Courage means doing the right thing—doing *God's thing*—no matter whether it's big or small, whether it's dramatic or ordinary, or whether it's noticed or unnoticed, or whether it's easy or terrifying. It means doing the right thing *no matter what*.

This is the kind of courage Roy Pontoh showed. This is the same kind of courage Julie Moore showed. And this very courage is required of *you* as warriors for Jesus. In today's world, we're surrounded with dangers, threats, pressures, and fears—and we need true courage to face them.

Point out the newsprint banner you've affixed on the wall and **SAY:**

There are lots of things out there in the world that cause Christians to live in fear instead of with courage. What are some fears and challenges that hold Christian teenagers back from living in courage for Jesus? Let's cover this graffiti wall with fears, challenges, or pressures that you think hold Christian teenagers back from living their faith boldly.

Invite everyone to gather around the graffiti wall and grab a marker. Encourage them to each start writing their thoughts and ideas all over the banner. They can write single words or phrases like "peer pressure" or detailed descriptions of situations or fears.

LEADER'S LOW-DOWN:

If teenagers need help thinking of fears and pressures to write down, use these prompts to help them brainstorm:

What are the biggest pressures Christian teens face that hold them back?

What negative things can happen to Christians if they stand up for their faith?

What are some temptations that the enemy uses to attack Christians and distract them from their mission?

What might Christian teenagers lose or have to give up in order to live boldly for Jesus?

What are some negative ways non-Christians talk about Christians? What are some negative ways they treat Christians?

What fears do you have that keep you from living as boldly as you should?

Have students keep writing until the banner is totally covered. Invite everybody to take a seat, then read several of the words and phrases on the banner aloud.

Then **SAY:** Let me share a quote with you that I think is another great way to define courage. Ambrose Redmoon said, "Courage is not the absence of fear, but rather the judgment that something else is more important than fear." In other words, courage means looking each of these fears straight in the eye, acknowledging their reality, and then deciding that something else is more important than them.

WANTED: COURAGE

SAY: In Scripture, God had a special message about courage for a man named Joshua.

Invite students to turn to Joshua 1:6–9 in their Bibles and have them follow along as you read:

"Be strong and courageous, because you will lead these people to inherit the land I swore to their forefathers to give them. Be strong and very courageous. Be careful to obey all the law my servant Moses gave you; do not turn from it to the right or to the left, that you may be successful wherever you go. Do not let this Book of the Law depart from your mouth; meditate on it day and night, so that you may be careful to do everything written in it. Then you will be prosperous and successful. Have I not commanded you? Be strong and courageous. Do not be terrified; do not be discouraged, for the LORD your God will be with you wherever you go."

ASK: What reasons does God give Joshua to be courageous? What truths from this passage can help us live in courage today?

SAY: This passage contains several important truths that help us live in courage. First, in verse 6, we see that God keeps His promises. Just like God kept His promise to Joshua, He also keeps His promises to us. Second, we are to live courageously because the all-powerful God of the universe commands it! Look at verse 9 again: "Have I not commanded you? Be strong and courageous." When the amazing, omnipotent Creator of the entire universe tells us to be courageous, we need to obey His orders. And most importantly, we can live in courage because God's got our back. At the end of verse 9, God says, "Do not be terrified; do not be discouraged, for the LORD your God will be with you wherever you go." We see this same idea repeated over and over again in Scripture.

Invite volunteers to read aloud Psalm 27:1–3, Isaiah 41:10, and Isaiah 43:1–5.

SAY: Did you catch that? God, the galaxy-crafter, planet-spinner, lightning bolt-maker *is with you* as you step into tough situations. He is present with you, at your side, to strengthen you and encourage you. We have no need to give in to fears when we know that God is with us. All fears pale in comparison to the knowledge of His presence and love.

Christians in the early church knew this reality in a deep way because they were persecuted severely for their faith. Some of the early Christians became *martyrs*—they were killed for their faith in Jesus. They had such tremendous courage that they'd rather die than recant their faith. Other early Christians were called *confessors*—this means that they were tortured (but not killed) for their faith. They were so courageous that they'd rather endure unbearable physical pain than backpedal about their faith.

This same situation is true for Christians in many parts of the world today. Like Roy Pontoh, Christians around the globe are tortured as confessors or even killed as martyrs because they will not renounce their faith in Jesus.

In our country, we don't face this same level of persecution and danger for our faith. But we *do* face persecution! We may not be physically tortured, but we can be socially isolated, made fun of, misunderstood, and even become social outcasts for our faith.

Let's take a little break for a news update. What might our schools look like if Christians did not stand up for what is right?

Play DVD clip "Nation Out of Control: Part 1" (Length 5:59)

SAY: We face . . . Then review aloud the fears and challenges students wrote on the graffiti wall.

SAY: It's interesting to look at the enemy's strategy here in America. When we think about dramatic moments like the one Roy faced, with someone threatening "renounce Jesus or I'll kill you," some of us may be pretty sure that we'd have the courage to do what Roy did. We believe that we'd be willing to stand up for our faith and pay the price. In that type of situation, the choice we must make is obvious.

But in America the enemy trips us up in much more subtle ways. Instead of sending an attacker who threatens us with death if we don't renounce our faith, the enemy whispers quiet messages in our ears like "Keep your faith quiet or someone will misunderstand you and make fun of you for it." Or "Don't stand up for Jesus because you'll lose some friends." Or "Don't tell your non-Christian friend about Jesus because you'll make her feel uncomfortable."

These subtle lies can cause us to live wimpy Christian lives instead of living boldly and courageously. We need to remember that courage isn't just about dramatic spotlight moments; real courage is doing God's thing even if it's small, undramatic, and unnoticed. It means being willing to undergo social ostracization if that's what it takes to follow Christ.

Let's see what's happening now at Dukakis High School.

Play DVD clip "Nation Out of Control: Part 2" (Length 4:47)

SAY: Have you ever felt like Grady did? Have you fallen prey to the enemy's whispers and lies? When have you let fears and pressures hold you back from living courageously—from doing God's thing no matter whether it's big or small, whether it's dramatic or plain, or whether it's noticed or unnoticed, or whether it's easy or terrifying?

SHORT SYNOPSIS:
"Nation Out of Control: Part 2"

As the saga at Dukakis High School continues, Grady, a popular Christian student, is faced with a tough choice: will he stand up for his faith or stay silent?

Play some music in the background and invite students to gather around the graffiti wall one more time and review all the fears written there. Explain that when they're ready, they should find a private space in the room and turn to page 24 in their Training Manual where they'll write about a recent time when they needed courage, but instead let fears hold them back. Remind them that whatever they write will be private, so they can be totally honest and candid. Tell students to take about 10 minutes to write.

WHEN I'VE LET FEAR WIN...

THE FEAR FACTOR

After 10 minutes for writing, invite everyone to gather back together.

SAY: We all know that we need courage. And we all know that at times it's just really hard to live out. What can we do to find courage when we're facing a tough situation? I want to share with you four principles for finding courage when we're facing fears and danger.

First, we find courage through prayer. When we're afraid, we can talk openly and honestly to God about our fear. There are some amazing examples of this in the Bible, such as Daniel praying when he was thrown into a den of hungry lions, or Esther, who prayed and fasted before risking her life to approach the king. And one really awesome example of this is David. We can find some of his brutally honest prayers about his fears in the book of Psalms.

Invite volunteers to read aloud Psalm 13:1–6 and 55:1–5.

SAY: David was totally honest with God about what he was feeling, and we can do the same. When we're afraid, we can tell God about it. We can name the pressures and dangers we're facing and we can ask God for help. True courage must be founded in prayer.

Second, we find courage through spending time with Jesus—not just through prayer, but also through reading Scripture and learning about Him. When we're close to Jesus, courage seems to rub off on us. Courage is simply a natural result of having a devoted relationship with Jesus. Let's see a great example of this in the Bible.

Invite a volunteer to read aloud Acts 4:13, then say:

People could *tell* the disciples had been with Jesus. They were bold and courageous and amazing, and everyone knew the reason. When we spend time with Jesus, we experience similar results— we are strengthened in our faith and emboldened to share our faith with the world.

Third, we find courage through the power of the Holy Spirit within us. Just as God promised Joshua that He would be with him, as Christians, we have the presence of God within us all the time. The Holy Spirit dwells inside of us and has power to help us face fears and challenges.

Invite volunteers to read aloud Mark 13:9–11, Romans 15:13, and 2 Timothy 1:6–8.

SAY: God gives us spiritual gifts, power, guidance, and the words to say through the Holy Spirit. When we are afraid, we need only remind ourselves that God dwells within us. What an amazing source of courage!

And last, we find courage by reminding ourselves of God's ultimate power and authority. Listen to what Jesus said in Matthew 10:28.

Invite a volunteer to read Matthew 10:28 aloud. Then **SAY:**

Here Jesus reminds us that every earthly fear is peanuts compared to the power God has regarding eternity. Humans may have the ability to threaten or even kill you, but they can *never, ever, ever* pull you away from God's love and His promise of eternal life. David understood this, as we see in Psalm 56.

Invite a volunteer to read aloud Psalm 56:3–4, then **SAY:**

David knew that humans couldn't do much to him in the scope of eternity. Yeah, they could possibly kill him, but *God* has authority over his soul. God has the power to create and maintain the entire universe. And with God on his side, why did he need to fear another person?

How do you want to grow in courage? What is God telling you right now? Turn to a partner and take some time to talk through your thoughts.

Invite partners to talk about these questions:

Which source of courage that we just learned about encourages you the most?
What are some other sources of courage for you?
What is one specific situation you are facing in which you need God to give you greater courage?

Prompt partners to pray for each other when they're done talking, asking God to help them both live as courageous warriors for Christ.

MINISTRY TIME

Dim the lights in your meeting area, then **SAY:**

We can live in courage. We can overcome the fears and challenges that hold us back. To represent our commitment to live in courage, we're going to tear down the fears on our graffiti wall. One at a time, I'd like you to come up and tear off part of the wall.

Once you've got your piece of the graffiti wall, take it with you and find a private spot where you can read and reflect on the Scriptures listed in your Training Manual on page 25. After you've finished reading, crumple your piece of paper into a ball and lay it at the foot of the cross, representing your commitment to surrender your fears to Him and live in courage. Then go back to your seat and pray about your commitment.

Lead teenagers in forming a single file line so that they can each tear down part of the graffiti wall. Then allow them about 10 minutes to read Scriptures and pray.

LEADER'S LOW-DOWN:

If large portions of the newsprint banner are left, just tear them up and place them at the foot of the cross.

MAKE IT REAL

With the lights still dimmed, **SAY:**

Most little kids are totally honest about their fears. And what are most of them afraid of? The dark. Sometimes all it takes is a tiny nightlight in a child's room to help him move past that fear and sleep in peace.

We live in a dark, dark world, crowded with fears and dangers and hunted by an enemy.

Light a candle; then **SAY:**

Yet we need not fear. We have the Light of truth! We have the Light of hope! We have the Light of the world—Jesus—on our side!

Pass around a basket containing candles (with drip guards) and have each student take one.

SAY: Psalm 27:1 says, "The Lord is my light and my salvation— whom shall I fear?" And the answer? We should fear no one. The Lord is our true light.

I'd like us to worship God by reminding each other of this awesome truth. I'll light some of your candles, and then I'd like you to pass the flame to each other so that each candle is lighted. When you pass your flame to someone, look them in the eye and say, "The Lord is your light!"

Turn to a student and say boldly, **"The Lord is your light!"** Then light his or her candle.

LEADER'S LOW-DOWN:

If you have a large group, light the candles of several students on the edges of the rows so that the process of passing the candle flame doesn't take as long.

LEADER'S LOW-DOWN:

If you're able, play the song "Whom Shall I Fear?" from Darrell Evans' album *Trading My Sorrows: The Best of Darrell Evans.* This upbeat worship song is drawn directly from Psalm 27.

When everyone has a lit candle, **SAY:**

Look around the room. When you're in a tough situation and you need courage, remember this moment. You are part of a community of faith. You are part of a body that is fighting for Jesus together. You are not alone. Let's pray.

Lead students in a concluding prayer, focusing on the courage they can find through prayer, through time with Jesus, through the Holy Spirit, and through trust in God's ultimate authority.

LEADER'S LOW-DOWN:

After this session, remove all the paper balls students placed at the foot of the cross.

RETREAT IS NOT AN OPTION

WHAT'S THE POINT?

True faith is defined by persistence and endurance—serving our King, day in and day out.

A QUICK GLANCE...

MINUTES	SECTION	SUPPLIES
up to 30	Optional Warm-Up Activity	Yarn, pieces of cardstock, pens, upbeat CD and CD player or instrumentalist
35 to 40	Faith that Digs Deep	Training Manuals, Bibles, pens, Dig In DVD, TV, DVD player
15 to 20	Faith that Doesn't Lapse	None
10 to 15	Faith Fertilizer	None
5 to 10	Deep-Rooted Faith	None
15 to 20	Ministry Time	Training Manuals, soil, plastic bins or shoe boxes, seeds, Worship CD and CD player or an instrumentalist, wooden cross up front
up to 15	Make It Real	CD player, Third Day's Offerings II CD, (Optional: a copy of Over the Edge: Ultimate Submission for each teen)

Before the event begins, make sure every teenager has their Training Manual. Set up a TV and DVD player and be ready to play the *Dig In* DVD. Also, set up a large, free-standing wooden cross near the front of your meeting area and ready a CD player with celebratory music as well as one with worshipful, instrumental music. Get a copy of Third Day's *Offerings II* CD; you'll play the song "Offering" at the conclusion of the session.

Get an 8 1/2 x 11 inch piece of cardstock for each student and use a hole punch to put two holes at the top of each piece. Loop a piece of yarn through the holes of each piece of cardstock so that students can "wear" the papers by putting the yarn around their neck. Last, get some seeds (such as pumpkin seeds or sunflower seeds) and fill plastic bins or shoeboxes with potting soil. You'll want approximately one bin or box filled with soil for every six to ten students. Set the boxes of soil in a circle at the foot of the wooden cross.

OPTIONAL WARM-UP ACTIVITY

Begin this final session of *Dig In* by coordinating an opportunity for students to celebrate their friendships by affirming and encouraging each other. Pass out the cardstock pieces you prepared so that each teenager gets one. Invite students to write their names at the top of their pieces of cardstock, then put them over their heads so they are hanging around their necks.

SAY: We've been through a lot during these last six sessions! We've had fun together, we've gotten to know each other, we've shared personal commitments, and we've prayed together. Let's take some time to celebrate what God has done in our lives by encouraging each other!

Explain that students should flip their cardstock sheets around so that they are hanging on their backs.

SAY: I'd like you to take 15 minutes to mingle with each other around the room, writing affirmations and encouraging messages on the papers on each other's backs. When you write a note on someone's back, you should either write one thing you really appreciate about that person, one positive personality trait that person has, or one way that their faith is inspiring to you. And don't sign your name—keep your encouragement anonymous.

There are two important rules for this activity: First, you must write meaningful encouraging things—this is not the time to joke around. Second, no one can look at what is written on their piece of paper until I say so. Got it?

Play upbeat, celebratory music and invite teenagers to begin mingling and writing. If some students are having a hard time letting others write on the papers on their back (for example, if they are extremely tall), let them know that they can temporarily take off their paper and hand it to others who want to write on it.

LEADER'S LOW-DOWN:

Set an example by participating in this activity yourself. Write sincere, personal notes on students' papers. The encouragement they receive during this activity will spur on their spiritual growth in significant ways!

LEADER'S LOW-DOWN:

If you have a large group, you may want to allow up to 25 minutes for students to write encouragements. This will allow time for teenagers to write meaningful notes for everyone in the group.

When the time is up, invite teenagers to find a private spot in the room and remove their papers. Prompt them to read all the notes written there and just enjoy a few minutes of soaking in all the love and affirmation they've received.

SAY: It's been awesome to go through these sessions with all of you. God has made each of you unique, and you're all very special to God and to me. I hope you keep your piece of paper and put it in a special place when you get home as a reminder of God's call on your life! Whenever you face tough times or need encouragement, just pull it out and read through these notes again to remind yourself of your true purpose—and your true value—in Christ.

FAITH THAT DIGS DEEP

SAY: OK, let's start off now with a little competition. We're going to play a game that is a test of endurance and perseverance. What I want you to do is get together with a partner and sit on the floor facing each other. When I say "go" your job is to make eye contact with your partner, keeping your eyes wide open and your expression totally blank. The challenge? You need to stare straight into your partner's eyes without blinking or cracking a smile. That's right; this is a good old-fashioned staring contest.

When everyone understands the game and they're ready to begin, **SAY:** Go! and allow up to two minutes if needed for all the pairs to compete.

ASK: Which of you smiled or blinked first?

After they've raised their hands, **SAY:**

Bad news . . . you're *out*. So, take a seat over on the side. Now the rest of you get to compete in Round Two. Find a new partner, and when I say "Go" you've got to try to out-stare each other again without blinking or smiling.

LEADER'S LOW-DOWN:

If you've got some amazing staring pairs in which neither blink or smile for three minutes straight, just declare it a tie and have both move on to the next round.

Have partners compete again, allowing up to two minutes if needed for all the pairs to compete. Again have all those who've lost sit on the side and have the winners form new pairs for another round. Continue this process until you've narrowed it down to one final winner (or a couple expert stare-ers!). Congratulate the winner(s) and lead the whole group in applauding.

After the activity, have everyone grab their Training Manual, their Bible, a pen, and a chair, and take a seat. (Have students create rows with their chairs, facing the front of the room.)

LEADER'S LOW-DOWN:

If your group is extremely large, just set a goal of playing until the game is narrowed down to five or ten winners instead of just one.

SAY: Wow, that was quite a test of persistence, endurance, and willpower! Sure, it wasn't the same kind of endurance required for something big like running a marathon, but in its own small way this challenge revealed some serious perseverance.

Today we're going to talk about endurance and perseverance in the little things *and* the big things. True endurance and persistence are the key marks of courage for the committed Christian.

Let's take a look at the story of Ethan Atherton. It took something out of the ordinary to teach him how to endure the tough things of life.

Play DVD clip "Taffy Bath" (Length 4:16)

SAY: It took a taffy bath for Ethan Atherton to learn endurance. Goofy and unrealistic, yes. But so often it can be really hard to endure in our faith. You may go home today excited and psyched to live out your mission as Christ's warrior. But how you choose to live a week from now, a month, a year . . . when the excitement fades,

SHORT SYNOPSIS: "Taffy Bath"

In classic Dr. Seuss-like style, this clip uses bright colors and goofy rhyming words to tell the story of a young man who finally learned to endure life's tough times.

that's the true test of a warrior. Let's take a look at the example of endurance the early Christians set for us.

Invite teenagers to turn to Hebrews 10 and be ready to follow along as you **SAY:**

The book of Hebrews is thought to be a sermon delivered to the house churches in Rome around 65 A.D., some 35 years after the death of Jesus. This was a time of heavy persecution for those who called themselves Christians. In chapter 10, we read some personal words of encouragement to a group of believers who seem to be wavering in their faith. Starting in v. 32 we read, "Remember those earlier days after you had received the light, when you stood your ground in a great contest in the face of suffering. Sometimes you were publicly exposed to insult and persecution; at other times you stood side by side with those who were so treated. You sympathized with those in prison and joyfully accepted the confiscation of your property, because you knew that you yourselves had better and lasting possessions." In Hebrews 12:4, we learn that though these particular Roman Christians "have not yet resisted to the point of shedding your blood," the author senses an imminent danger. In 12:12, he encourages them, "strengthen your feeble arms and weak knees." So much of the Bible concerns this same theme: Endurance! Perseverance!

Think about what these followers of Jesus were going through—suffering, public mockery, persecution, confiscation of their personal property, prison! Things were tough for these early Christians. How were they able to hold on?

These courageous Jesus-followers had this kind of amazing perseverance because their faith wasn't merely superficial; they had a true, rooted, and grounded faith. Jesus explained the type of faith characterized by perseverance and endurance in one of His most famous parables. Let's read it together.

Invite a volunteer to read aloud Matthew 13:1–9, 18–23 while everyone else reads along in their own Bibles.

SAY: This parable explains perfectly the difference between superficial faith and a deep, long-lasting faith. I'd like you to get together in groups of three or four and study this parable, discussing what you think it means and how it applies to modern times.

When students form small groups, have them turn to pages 26–27 in their Training Manuals. Give them about 10 minutes to talk through the discussion questions, then have everyone gather back together.

Ask volunteers to share their group's answers for each of these questions from the Training Manual page.

ASK: According to this passage, what is superficial faith?

What's a modern example of the first type of seed that's snatched up by birds?

What's an example you came up with for the second kind of seed that landed on shallow soil?

What about an example of the seed that sprouts among thorns?

What other factors can cause teenagers today to have a "shallow" or superficial faith?

Affirm the ideas teenagers shared, then **SAY:**

Let's focus for a moment on the seed that fell on rocky soil. Jesus described it this way in 13:20–21: "What was sown on rocky places is the man who hears the word and at once receives it with joy. But since he has no root, he lasts only a short time. When trouble or persecution comes because of the world, he quickly falls away." Now think about this for a moment . . . does this ever describe *your faith*? Have you found yourself experiencing mountain-top moments of faith—times when you responded to God with great joy—only later to discover that your excitement, your commitment, has withered away? When tough times came your way, when the influence of non-Christian friends, or when your own habits of sin caused your enthusiasm to subside, were your commitments forgotten? And before you knew it, you were back to living the same way things *used* to be?

This is the danger of shallow faith, and it can creep up on any of us! Spiritual "highs" can give us the illusion of strong faith, but if our roots are only shallow—if they don't dig deep—we simply won't make it through trials and persecution. We won't have the endurance and perseverance modeled by the early Christians in Hebrews 10.

FAITH THAT DOESN'T LAPSE . . .

SAY: In our last session I told you about two types of Christians in the early church: martyrs and confessors. *Martyrs* were Christians who were killed because they wouldn't renounce their faith in Jesus. *Confessors* were Christians who weren't killed, but who did endure serious persecution—including physical torture—for their faith. These martyrs and confessors were like the deep-rooted seeds in Jesus' parable. They persevered through terrible trials because they had a grounded, solid faith.

But in the early church, there was another type of Christian: the *lapsi*. *Lapsi* was the Latin term given to Christians who recanted their faith. Like the shallow-rooted plant, when push came to shove they gave up their faith in Jesus rather than suffer for it. There were two types of *lapsi*—those who immediately gave up their faith when they were threatened with hardship, and those who tried to hold out but eventually wavered as the crowds ridiculed them.

Okay, now picture this for a minute. Imagine a room filled with confessors—those who had been tortured for their faith. They might be missing eyes, limbs, and fingers as a result of what they went through. And in walks a fellow Christian—*a lapsi*—who publicly gave up his faith because he was afraid of pain and ridicule. The *lapsi* is completely unharmed—no scars, no missing fingers. He's perfectly healthy. Imagine how guilty he must have felt when he looked around him and the contrast was so sharp between his shallow faith and the deep-rooted faith of his friends. Imagine the challenge of the confessors as they attempted to forgive their friend.

The truth of the matter is that there are countless *"lapsi"* Christians today, but we'd use a different term: we'd say they have "lapsed" in their faith. Countless people call themselves Christians—and they do sincerely believe in many of the ideas of Christianity. But when tough times come—when push comes to shove—they're not willing to lose anything for their faith . . . so they give it up.

ASK the group: **How does the idea of *lapsi* Christians compare with the way Christians today "lapse" in their faith?**

What types of circumstances could cause a Christian teenager to give up his or her faith or hide it from others?

SAY: When we think about our own faith commitment, it's helpful to think in terms of the categories of Christians in the early church: martyrs and confessors, or *lapsi*. Because of the serious persecution they faced, there really wasn't a middle ground. Each Christian eventually had to choose: "Will I live boldly for my faith, no matter what the cost? Or will I give in to fear, to pressure, to danger when the moment of decision comes?"

We each need to face that question ourselves. Will the way we live confess and proclaim our faith? Or will we lapse into the ways of the world whenever we face stress, pressure, or danger?

I'd like you to close your eyes for a moment. I am going to ask you some questions and I want you to quietly think about what they mean to you. Your thoughts are completely private: just between you and God.

When everyone has closed their eyes, ask students these questions, allowing about one minute of silence after each one:

Is your level of faith commitment the same as a martyr or confessor? If not, why not?

When have circumstances, pressures, or fears caused you to lapse in your faith?

What would it look like for you on an everyday basis to live like a martyr or a confessor?

Are you willing to commit to boldly following Jesus, no matter the cost? If so, pray about it now.

FAITH FERTILIZER

Invite everyone to open their eyes and get out their Bibles again.

SAY: Let's return to the parable of the seeds. The final type of seed was different from the rest.

Invite a volunteer to read aloud Matthew 13:8 and another to read aloud Matthew 13:23.

SAY: This enduring faith is what God wants for each of us. Like a seed in fertile soil, our faith can develop deep, strong roots that nourish us and keep us strong no matter what danger or persecution we face. But how does a person develop this type of faith? Is it just a matter of luck—the idea that some people are prone to have strong faith and others to have weak faith? I don't think so. God's Word is clear that there are several things we can do— several essential spiritual practices—that send our roots deep. These practices become like "faith fertilizer," nourishing us and helping us take root. As we develop these habits and make them an essential part of our everyday lives, we develop faith that endures and perseveres, no matter what.

The first important faith fertilizer is investing regular time in God's Word. When we develop habits of studying Scripture, memorizing meaningful passages, and meditating on specific verses, our faith goes deeper. The psalmist David put it this way: "I have hidden your word in my heart that I might not sin against you" (Psalm 119:11). Now let's face it: just listening to sermons or youth group talks doesn't cut it. Sure, you *hear* truths from God's Word, but are you *hiding them in your heart?* Are you spending enough time in God's Word for it to implant itself in the center of your being? To truly grow in faith, we must spend regular, habitual time on our own, individually reading God's Word and applying it to our lives.

A second critical faith fertilizer is prayer. Prayer, in its most elemental form, essentially means talking and listening to God. You don't need to say anything special or spiritual sounding—just share your heart with God and ask Him to share His heart with you. And prayer shouldn't be something we do just when we want something, as if God were a spiritual Santa Claus. Prayer is how we build our friendship with God; through prayer, we get to know God better and we strengthen our connection with Him. By listening to the Holy Spirit in prayer, we can hear His quiet voice convicting us of sin or prompting us to share our faith. The Apostle Paul set the standard high; in 1 Thessalonians 5:17 he said, "pray continually." This means we can pray *all the time*. During any moment, any situation, we can speak to God in our hearts. When we understand the importance of prayer in our daily lives and put it into practice, our faith roots grow deep.

Christian friendships are another essential faith fertilizer. God doesn't want us to be lone-ranger Christians, out on our own in the world. He has designed us to be part of a body, a family of believers who strengthen and encourage each other in faith. To really grow strong in our faith, each of us needs to nourish sincere friendships with other Christians. In those relationships, we can encourage and affirm each other. Remember the encouragement you received from our Warm-Up Activity? Imagine getting that level of encouragement day after day! When we seek to help each other in faith by engaging in spiritual friendships, the impact we can have on each other is phenomenal. If you want to give your faith-growth a boost, ask a Christian friend to hold you accountable. Tell each other about your struggles and your desire to grow. Be willing to ask and answer hard questions. Pray for each other!

Along those same lines, another key faith fertilizer is commitment to corporate worship. Corporate worship simply means gathering for worship and teaching with other Christians. If you want to really grow in your faith, you need to make sure you're committed to your church. Make it a priority to attend Sunday morning services where you'll learn from God's Word together and you'll worship God with the rest of your church family. When we're committed to a church body, we grow! That's how God made us.

There are many other Christian practices that can help you grow in faith, but I've focused here on four of the essential practices that will help your faith take root: studying Scripture, praying continually, fellowship with Christian friends, and participation in a local church. When you make these practices a priority in your life, your faith will strengthen and grow. You'll be able to persevere through trials and persecution; you'll endure the test of time.

DEEP-ROOTED FAITH

SAY: Let me tell you the story of a man with a deep-rooted faith. Throughout the first three centuries things would only get worse for Christians living in the Roman world, and especially for those in Rome. Matthew was martyred in 60 A.D. James (the less) in 66. Peter and Paul fell about the same time. About 100 years later the situation continued to worsen for Christians. Tradition tells us that Polycarp, a elderly man who had been a student of the apostle John, when captured was asked to "reproach Christ." Polycarp responded by saying, "Eighty and six years have I served Him, and He never once wronged me;

how then shall I blaspheme my King, Who hath saved me?"[12] He was then tied to a stake and sticks were placed at its base. The wood was set on fire, and the flames rose up around him. What was Polycarp doing as the blazing fire surrounded him? Singing praises to God! The executioner then pierced Polycarp with a sword. So much blood poured out that it put out the fire. Yet 'til his last breath, Polycarp was praising Jesus. What *astonishing* courage!

Polycarp is an amazing example of perseverance. Not only was he faithful throughout his unbelievably painful execution, but did you catch what Polycarp said? He said, "I've served Christ for 86 years!" Polycarp walked in dedicated faith with Jesus for nearly nine decades! Here is the true portrait of perseverance—not just that he was faithful in the dramatic moment of martyrdom, but that he was also faithful in his day-to-day life . . . for 86 years.

Yes, true Christian courage is found in the "big moments" of life—when we're given opportunities to publicly take a stand for our faith or when we're faced with persecution and we stand the test. But true Christian courage and endurance is also found in the "little moments"—in the humble living out of our faith in everyday life. It's the courage of praying daily, of studying Scripture, of caring for those in need. It's the courage of befriending outcasts, showing kindness, and having the boldness to forgive. It's the courage of telling others about Jesus and doing what's right, even if nobody else sees. It's the courage that lasts 86 years, and keeps on going through the final moments of life on earth. It's the courage that knows retreat is not an option, in the big moments *or* the little moments.

MINISTRY TIME

Invite students to form pairs and turn to page 28 in their Training Manuals. Ask them to take about 10 minutes to talk through the questions together.

DEEP-ROOTED FAITH

TALK ABOUT THESE QUESTIONS TOGETHER:

What is your response to Polycarp's story? What about it stands out most to you?

Which is the more amazing feat—being martyred for his faith or living faithfully for 86 years?

When you think of the course of your own life and imagine yourself in your 80s or 90s, what do you want your faith to be like? Describe it.

What steps do you need to take now to build toward that kind of faith in your old age?

Review the "Faith Fertilizers" in the margin box. Are there additional faith fertilizers that are meaningful to you? How do they help you grow?

In which of these areas do you need to grow in order to have a deep-rooted faith? Commit to God and pray with your partner about developing one area in the immediate future.

FAITH FERTILIZERS
Regular time in the Bible
Regular time in prayer
Christian friendship (encouragement, accountability)
Involvement in corporate worship

NOW take a moment to think through the themes and ideas of the past seven sessions. (Feel free to flip through this Training Manual to remind yourself.) How would you sum up the main spiritual growth steps you want to take now that we've concluded DIG IN?

28   DIG IN

During this discussion, students will reflect on the story of Polycarp, considering both his daily courage and his courage in his final moment. They'll discuss their own vision for their lives—what do they want their faith to be like when they're in their 80s or 90s? What can they do now to start building towards that goal? In pairs students will also review the "Faith Fertilizer" Christian practices and talk about areas in which they need to grow in order to deepen their faith.

After 10 minutes, pass around bags of seeds, instructing each student to take one seed.

SAY: Take a moment to pray with your partner about your specific desire to fertilize your faith. Then come together to the cross where you'll find boxes of soil. Plant your seed deep in the soil to symbolize the lifelong, unwavering faith you want for yourself. When you're done, return to your seat in an attitude of prayer.

Play worshipful music in the background while students pray and plant seeds.

LEADER'S LOW-DOWN:

During this act of symbolism, pray for the students in your youth group. Ask God to make planting the seed a meaningful metaphor—something they'll remember for the rest of their lives.

MAKE IT REAL

When all have returned to their seats, **SAY:**

Continue in a prayer mind-set as I read you a passage from Scripture.

Read aloud Matthew 14:22–33.

SAY: Imagine this scene. The windstorm is churning a large body of water. The disciples are clinging to a boat in this windstorm. They see a figure walking toward them *on the water*. They are absolutely terrified. The figure calls out, "Take courage! It is I. Don't be afraid." Yet the disciples are still confused—is it really Him? Is it really Jesus?

Then Peter takes that amazing, unbelievable, unreal step of courage. He literally puts his foot over the side of the boat and plants it right in the water. Imagine the guts it took to take that step! Imagine the instinctive and rational fears he overcame to do it! And Peter's foot is buoyed . . . it stays on top of the water! Peter begins to walk toward Jesus!

But soon the raging waves and howling winds catch his eye. Whoa! This is getting dangerous. The circumstances around him draw his attention. His legs start to wobble—he starts to feel afraid. And in that moment, when the waves around him fill him with fear and doubt, he starts to sink.

Jesus is right there. He grabs hold of Peter and pulls him up. Jesus leads Peter back to the boat and they step on board. The disciples, especially Peter, are astounded. They believe that Jesus is the Son of God!

What conclusion can we draw from this true story? One important point for us is that there's a lot more to faith than dramatic first steps. When we get pumped up after a Christian event or when we're on a mountain top, we feel ready to take big dramatic steps of faith. We make commitments and we feel bold and courageous about following through with them. Some of you may feel that way right now as you think about the commitments you've made to God during our sessions. Like Peter did, we're eager and excited to take big steps. Yet, like Peter did, we soon let circumstances and fears distract us. Somehow, we stop walking . . . somehow our commitments sink.

The real test of faith isn't in the first step . . . it's in the next one . . . and the next one . . . and the next one . . . and the next one . . . and the next one. True courage is found in putting one foot in front of the other, *continuing* to walk out our faith, enduring despite circumstances. The waves will keep beating and foaming around us. We'll be farther and farther from safety. But the courage of true faith involves endurance and persistence: a commitment to keep taking those steps, putting one foot right after the other.

We've been through a lot together during these last seven sessions. We've explored the meaning of true devotion. We've discovered our calling to defy the enemy. We've been charged with our mission in this world. We've committed to live in courage and perseverance.

But our journey isn't over. *Over the Edge: Ultimate Submission* is a powerful tool that I challenge you to use to help you take the next step, and the next one, and the next one, and the next one.

Hold up a sample copy.

SAY: This discipleship journal will help you explore more of each of the themes we discussed. As part of your daily personal time with God, you'll dig into the Bible, commune with God in prayer, and apply God's truths to your life. I urge you to commit to take on this challenge—to take each daily step by committing to go through this journal for the next seven weeks. Are you up for the challenge?

LEADER'S LOW-DOWN:

Over the Edge: Ultimate Submission is a valuable tool for teens as they go back to the true battlefield of their daily lives. If you purchased a copy for each student, you will have a chance to hand them out at the end of this session.

If resources are limited, you will want to give students and their parents the opportunity to purchase this self-discipleship journal. You will find a reproducible letter to parents online at http://downloads.battlecry.com.

As we conclude our time together, I want us to wrap up by listening to a song. The lyrics of this song by Third Day sum up the entire theme of *Dig In*, saying, "The only thing that I can give You is the life You gave to me." Let's gather around the cross as we listen to the words. You can stand or kneel. You can open your eyes or close them. In whatever posture you'd like, listen to the song and let the words become your prayer.

Play the song "Offering" from Third Day's *Offerings II* CD. Then conclude the session by giving a copy of *Over the Edge: Ultimate Submission* to each teen.

1 uscis.gov/graphics/services/natz/oath.htm (accessed October 2005).

2 Accounts of the disciples' deaths according to church tradition can be found in *Foxe's Book of Martyrs*, Grand Rapids: Zondervan Publishing House, 1926. Several revised and updated versions of this text are also available.

3 The text of this Public Domain hymn can be found at http://www.cyberhymnal.org/htm/o/n/onwardcs.htm (accessed October 2005).

4 http://www.usacitiesonline.com/mottosa-b.htm (accessed October 2005).

5 The quote describing Jesus' crucifixion can be found at http://www.ourcatholicfaith.org/crucifixion.html (accessed October 2005).

6 This Public Domain hymn text is excerpted from *Hymns for the Family of God*. Nashville: Paragon Associates, Inc., 1976.

7 Adapted from http://news.nationalgeographic.com/news/2005/06/0610_050610_tv_mafia.html (accessed October 2005).

8 G.K. Chesterton's *Orthodoxy*. San Francisco: Ignatius Press, 1908 (page 84).

9 Caedmon's Call CD *Caedmon's Call*, "This World" (Track 4).

10 Adapted from *Jesus Freaks* by DC Talk and The Voice of the Martyrs. Tulsa: Albury Publishing, 1999 (pages 47-48).

11 Adapted from http://www.christianitytoday.com/cl/2000/005/6.52.html (accessed October 2005).

12 Quote from *Foxe's Book of Martyrs* (Public Domain). Published in Grand Rapids: Zondervan Publishing House, 1926.

OVER THE EDGE: ULTIMATE SUBMISSION

Over the Edge: Ultimate Submission is a huge part of what makes *Dig In* such a unique, impactful experience for teens! Most curriculums hit the issues hard but fail to follow up with teens. Without repetition, most information is forgotten within days or even hours, and teens never experience substantial life change. *Over the Edge* overcomes this. Teens will spend the seven weeks following *Dig In* diving even deeper into the lessons they've learned. They'll go beyond theories of discipleship and really begin living the life God has designed for them!

You can order a copy of the *Over the Edge: Ultimate Submission* for each member of your youth group at Battlecry.com. Or you may give students and their parents the opportunity to purchase this valuable resource. You can download a parents' letter at http://downloads.battlecry.com (be sure to fill in your specific information). This letter gives purchasing details and explains the benefits teens experience by going through *Over the Edge: Ultimate Submission.*

While *Over the Edge: Ultimate Submission* is designed to be uniquely personal for each youth, students benefit big time from accountability. Following along in this self-discipleship journal yourself will allow you to keep up on the specific basic training issues your youth are revisiting daily. Additionally, you can continue a group discussion every week during youth group, Sunday school, or small group times. Below you will find each week's memory verse and weekly questions that correspond with *Over the Edge: Ultimate Submission.* You may choose to use these questions in a number of ways:

• Ask the questions out loud to your entire group to spur discussion.

• Write each question for that week on small slips of paper (one question per slip); have each student draw a slip from a hat, get together with all other teens who have the same question, and discuss it within this newly formed small group.

• Write that week's questions on a whiteboard or large sheet of paper; give each teen a blank piece of paper and a pencil; have teens write their favorite question or a question of their own on their sheet of paper; have teens crumple their paper into a "snow-ball;" teens toss their "snowballs" around the room while music plays; when the music stops, teens pick up the "snowball" nearest them and answer the question on the paper either in writing or in discussion.

• Write several questions each week on a large sheet of butcher paper, divide your group into pairs, and have each pair choose one question to discuss.

• Divide your group into five groups (if your group is larger than 30, you may want to divide your group into more than five; limit subgroups to six people); assign a question to each small group; once small groups have discussed their question they report back to the large group.

WEEK ONE: MORE THAN WORDS

Memory Verse:

That if you confess with your mouth, "Jesus is Lord," and believe in your heart that God raised him from the dead, you will be saved.
—Romans 10:9

Questions to ask your group:

Why is it important to us that the King is in charge?

In your everyday life, what does it look like to be obedient to God?

In what ways do you think you need to be bolder in following Jesus? What steps can you take to achieve this boldness?

For each of the following pieces of spiritual armor, list one way you can actively use it in your everyday life: Belt of Truth, Breastplate of Righteousness, Feet Fitted with Readiness, Shield of Faith, Helmet of Salvation, Sword of the Spirit.

What type of role do you picture yourself having in God's army? How can you see yourself carrying out that role every day?

WEEK TWO: LOVE IN ACTION

Memory Verse:

"Love the Lord your God with all your heart and with all your soul and with all your mind and with all your strength." The second is this: "Love your neighbor as yourself." There is no commandment greater than these.
—Mark 12:30–31

Questions to ask your group:

Jesus tells us to "love your neighbor as your-self." What does this really mean? What should it look like in our daily lives?

In Ezekiel 11:19, the Lord talked about the Israelites: "I will give them an undivided heart." What does it mean to have an "undivided heart"?

How can you be obedient with each of the following: your heart and soul, your mind, and your strength?

During *Dig In*, we talked about showing our love for God in every area of our lives. How are you showing love in each of these areas: time, money, schoolwork, family relationships, hobbies, friend relationships, dreams, dating relationships, and life?

On a scale of 1–10 (1 being super hard, 10 being super easy), how easy is it to love God? Why is that? How easy is it to love others? Why?

WEEK THREE:
I'M YOURS
Memory Verse:
Then Jesus said to his disciples, "If anyone would come after me, he must deny himself and take up his cross and follow me."
—Matthew 16:24

Questions to ask your group:
God wants us to be symbols of Him. How can you better carry out your role as His symbol?

How does it make you feel that Jesus would go to the cross on purpose and on your behalf?

God is all-powerful. So why do you think He chose to sacrifice His Son?

If you choose to tell Jesus, "I'm Yours forever," what will your life be like now and in the future?

What does it mean for you to deny yourself and take up your cross?

WEEK FOUR:
NAMING THE ENEMY
Memory Verse:
Everyone who does evil hates the light, and will not come into the light for fear that his deeds will be exposed.
—John 3:20

Questions to ask your group:
What is the difference between *believing that Jesus died* on the cross for our sins and *putting faith* in the fact?

How does God feel about you? How does Satan feel about you? How do you feel about God? How do you feel about Satan?

Think about some gray areas in your life. What could you do to get rid of these? Name some tactics to ensure that your mind dwells on "whatever is true, whatever is noble, whatever is right, whatever is pure, whatever is lovely, whatever is admirable" (Phil. 4:8).

What can you do in your daily life to cultivate a crazy-in-love-with-Jesus kind of love?

You will experience temptation, but God promises to provide a way for you to "stand up under it" (1 Cor. 10:13). What are some ways that you have resisted temptation in the past? What are some additional ways that you could use in the future?

WEEK FIVE:
HERE WE ARE
Memory Verse:
Now this is our boast: Our conscience testifies that we have conducted ourselves in the world, and especially in our relations with you, in the holiness and sincerity that are from God. We have done so not according to worldly wisdom but according to God's grace.
—2 Corinthians 1:12

Questions to ask your group:
What are three actions you can take to show others that you are "set apart" from the world?

What does the phrase, "Hate the sin; love the sinner," mean to you? How can you put that phrase into practice in your daily life at school, at home, or with your friends?

Think of a time in your life when you did not feel at home in the world. Describe this time to a friend.

How does the way you live your life show others *who* God is?

Is it more, less, or equally important to *tell about Jesus* as compared to *showing Him* through the way you live your life? Why?

WEEK SIX: THE RED BADGE OF COURAGE

Memory Verse:

Be strong and courageous. Do not be afraid or terrified because of them, for the Lord your God goes with you; he will never leave you nor forsake you.
—Deuteronomy 31:6

Questions to ask your group:

How would you define a courageous Christian?

How can you be courageous for God at school? at home? with your friends?

What differences do you see in your life during times when you're actively reading your Bible versus times when God's Word has been sitting on your shelf for a while?

If you were able to act courageously—with the Holy Spirit as your guide—what effect do you think you could have on those around you?

Think of a time over the past seven weeks that's been pretty tough for you. How did you respond? If you were to go through it again, would you respond differently? Why or why not?

WEEK SEVEN: DEEP ROOTS

Memory Verse:

I have hidden your word in my heart that I might not sin against you.
—Psalm 119:11

Questions to ask your group:

Look up Proverbs 13:20. What does this verse say about how the people you hang with will have an effect on your understanding and wisdom?

Think of a time in your life when it was challenging for you to stay close to Jesus. What made it challenging? Share about this time with a friend in the room.

Why is it wrong to worry? What can you do to keep from worrying?

Read Matthew 13:8. What are some things you can do to keep your soil rich and productive?

Think of a time when someone encouraged you when you were feeling down. Share about this time with someone sitting near you. Now think of someone you could encourage this week. Now go do it!